KEY
WOMEN
WRITERS
EDITOR: SUE ROE

# GEORGE ELIOT

D0862690

KEY
WOMEN
WRITERS
EDITOR: SUE ROE

# GEORGE ELIOT

## GILLIAN BEER

Indiana University Press
Bloomington

Manufactured in Great Britain

**Library of Congress Cataloging-in-Publication Data**

Beer, Gillian.
  George Eliot.

  Bibliography: p.
  1. Eliot, George, 1819–1880—Criticism and
interpretation.    I. Title.
PR4688.B34   1986        823'.8        85-45958
ISBN 0-253-30100-9
ISBN 0-253-25450-7 (pbk.)

1 2 3 4 5 90 89 88 87 86

For John Beer

# Titles in the Key Women Writers Series

# Key Women Writers
## Series Editor: Sue Roe

The *Key Women Writers* series has developed in a spirit of challenge, exploration and interrogation. Looking again at the work of women writers with established places in the mainstream of the literary tradition, the series asks, in what ways can such writers be regarded as feminist? Does their status as canonical writers ignore the notion that there are ways of writing and thinking which are specific to women? Or is it the case that such writers have integrated within their writing a feminist perspective which so subtly maintains its place that these are writers who have, hitherto, been largely misread?

In answering these questions, each volume in the series is attentive to aspects of composition such as style and voice, as well as to the ideas and issues to emerge out of women's writing practice. For while recent developments in literary and feminist theory have played a significant part in the creation of the series, feminist theory represents no specific methodology, but rather an opportunity to broaden our range of responses to the issues of history, pyschology and gender which have always engaged women writers. A new and creative dynamics between a woman critic and her female subject has been made possible by recent developments in feminist theory, and the series seeks to reflect the important critical insights which have emerged out of this new, essentially feminist, style of engagement. It is not always the case that literary theory can be directly transposed from its sources in other disciplines to the practice of reading writing by women. The series investigates the possibility that a distinction may need to be made between feminist politics and the literary criticism of women's writing which has not, up to now, been sufficiently emphasized. Feminist reading, as well as feminist writing, still needs to be constantly interpreted and re-interpreted. The complexity and range of choices implicit in this procedure are represented throughout the series. As works of criticism, all the volumes in the series represent wide-ranging and creative styles of discourse, seeking at all times to express the particular resonances and perspectives of individual women writers.

*Sue Roe*

# Contents

The attempt of the 'prelude' and the final chapter to represent the book as an elaborate contribution to the 'Woman's' question, seems to us a mistake.

(R.H. Hutton, review of *Middlemarch*, 1872)

The ancient consciousness of woman, charged with suffering and sensibility, and for so many ages dumb, seems in them to have brimmed and overflowed and uttered a demand for something—they scarcely know what—

(Virginia Woolf, on George Eliot's heroines, 1919)

Who would not have some purpose in life as independent in its value as art is to the artist?

(Marian Evans/[George Eliot], 'From the Notebook of an Eccentric' (1846) her first published prose)

# Preface

In writing this study I have been grateful for the resources of the Cambridge University Library, the English Faculty Library and the Bodleian Library, Oxford. But I have been most particularly happy to have the opportunity to use the research resources of our own college library at Girton. Working with the Blackburn Collection of nineteenth-century documents on the women's movement, the Bodichon collection, the new collection of Bessie Rayner Parkes letters, and the excellent general stock of nineteenth-century books made me appreciate afresh the continuing intellectual richness of our institution. I regret only that the small scale of the present work cannot do justice to the available material. I would like to thank Margaret Gaskell, the Girton Librarian, for her help and generosity.

Barbara Norden and other members of my seminar on 'Women and Education, 1840–70' provided the stimulus of discussion, as did Sally Shuttleworth, and Kate Perry, Archivist of the Parkes collection. I have also learnt a lot from the English Faculty seminars, organized by Lisa Jardine, on the 'Literary Representation of Women'. Dagmar Diestel checked the typescript most conscientiously, and Jean Smith helped by typing the bibliography even when she was already hard pressed. Poppy Holden and the Cambridge Consort of Viols made

me think anew about the significance of voice and music
in George Eliot's work and I am grateful to them for this
and much else.

Gillian Beer
Girton College,
Cambridge

All references to George Eliot's works in the text are to
the Cabinet edition. Chapter references are provided for
the convenience of readers working with other editions.
Full details of all books cited by surname, date and page
reference in the text can be found in the bibliography.

Chapter One

# The 'Woman's Question'

## I

There are many ways of studying George Eliot. The general title of this series allows us to ask questions about her art which, though they may not be new, have a new emphasis for us. I have seen my task here as being the study of the novels in the light of their being produced by a woman. That woman helped in some measure to bring into question assumptions about male/female polarisations, about woman, and about the awkwardly pre-emptive forms 'womanly' and 'womanhood'. Her presence at the centre of literary culture in the past hundred years is of immense worth to other women, and her achievement can be belittled only at our own cost. Her writing, by being written, casts doubt on characteristics according to gender or to social place. Yet she was not, according to our lights, either a feminist theorist or activist. She persistently worked at the central dilemmas of feminism in her time without

1

setting out to write feminist novels. She probed current assumptions about 'women's nature' as well as scrutinising the arguments of her friends in the women's movement. She saw men and women as locked together by their needs and hopes, and by their common misunderstanding. In order to assess more fully the nature and difficulties of her achievement, I shall analyse the novels and some of the poetry not only in the light of recent criticism but also in relation to other Victorian writing, especially that concerned with the 'nature' of women and with their social position.

Words on the page are not autonomous. They are connected within the text by means of grammatical structures, narrative trajectories, and by the erased needs of the writer. Beyond that, they are also controlled and extended by their part in current controversies, and may have a combative significance which vanishes as ideological conditions change.

One of the most misleading bequeathments of the nineteenth century is the widespread assumption that systems of explanation must necessarily register growth as well as change, accumulation as well as shifts of attention. Anyone who has studied women's movements and the discussion of women's rights and positions knows well that there has been no steady arc of progress. Instead, arguments and determinations have been advanced and then have apparently vanished again, as we see in the relationship between the end of the eighteenth century with the complex arguments of Mary Hays and Mary Wollstonecraft, and the beginning of the nineteenth. We need to beware of misreading the meaning of acts and statements after conditions have changed. What may have a correct emphasis at one political moment may need to be jettisoned ten years later, or would properly have been repudiated ten years earlier.

Equally, we should not fall into the trap of seeing earlier movements merely as proto-feminism, something disposable and insignificant, allowing us to praise current theory and practice in its post-causal absolutism as if no feminist awareness had existed before twenty years from our own privileged moment. In writing this study I have been grateful both for the resources of recent theory and for the documents of the Victorian women's movement. I have also borne in mind that narrative question in *Middlemarch*: 'But why always Dorothea?' I hope that I have avoided that form of ghetto which implies that only women are fit topic for women, and also that style of commentary which returns all creativity solely to women's psychosexual problems.

George Eliot has been a knot of controversy for feminist critics. The scale and scope of her achievement is undeniable: the intellectual depth of connected life, the emotional power of humdrum experience, the range of exploratory discourses. What is debated is the relation of that achievement to our needs as women and her powers as a woman. One key problem has been the obduracy with which she encloses her heroines within the confines of ordinary possibility, confines from which the author had, by means of her writing, escaped. Related to this is the frequency with which renunciation is discovered as a good, particularly in her early writing. Françoise Basch writes that ' "Renunciation", for George Eliot, is the essence of virtue; and it is the chief moral reality implied by her whole outlook' (Basch, 1974, p.97). One of her women admirers, after reading her poem, 'The Spanish Gypsy' in 1869, wrote to her: 'Must noble women always fail? Is there no sumptuous flower of happiness for us?' (Haight, 1978, viii. p.463). Yet George Eliot mocks renunciation's virtue in other novelists,

3

returns again and again to it as problem, not as satisfaction, and writes into her work women who claim, and writing which grasps, the prize of fullness. The first wave of recent feminist literary theory gave short shrift to George Eliot. Kate Millett had only this to say:

> 'Living in sin', George Eliot lived the revolution as well perhaps, but she did not write of it. She is stuck with the Ruskinian service ethic and the pervasive Victorian fantasy of the good woman who goes down into Samaria and rescues the fallen man—nurse, guide, mother, adjunct of the race. Dorothea's predicament in *Middlemarch* is an eloquent plea that a fine mind be allowed an occupation; but it goes no further than petition. She marries Will Ladislaw and can expect no more of life than the discovery of a good companion whom she can serve as secretary. (Millett, 1972, p.139)

Millett's objection is that George Eliot does not offer a positive model for aspirant women, but simply represents their curtailment. The argument that representation of the status quo may serve to reinforce the status quo cannot lightly be dismissed, though in *Middlemarch*, as I shall show, George Eliot employs the double time-scheme of the novel to disturb any temptation to accept what is represented as either desirable or absolute. Zelda Austen sees the distrust of George Eliot as linked to a refusal of formalism in this phase of American feminist writing: 'Feminist critics uniformly resist making judgements about literature on the basis of style, structure, or mimesis' (Austen, 1976, p.554).

Since the work of Gilbert and Gubar (1979), Nancy Miller (1980), and Elizabeth Ermarth (1983) that criticism is less apt, though there is still a gap between the formal preoccupations of French critics such as Kristeva and Cixous, and the moralised, character-oriented writing of much American and Anglo-Saxon criticism. The most vivid attack on George Eliot in those terms is Ellen Moers' where she argues that 'George Eliot . . . was no feminist':

> Dinah Morris gives up her preaching career at the end of *Adam Bede* with a flutter of glad submission, for George Eliot, as her readers have always been surprised to discover, was no feminist. That is, her aim as a novelist was not to argue for a diminishing of the social inhibitions and a widening of the options that affects the lives of ordinary women; instead, like Mme de Stäel, George Eliot was always concerned with the superior, large-souled woman whose distinction resides not in her deeds but in her capacity to attract attention and arouse admiration . . . Dorothea Brooke in *Middlemarch* . . . is good for nothing *but* to be admired. An arrogant, selfish, spoiled, rich beauty, she does but little harm in the novel. (Moers, 1978, p.194)

The energetic perversity of this judgement certainly draws attention to the problem of the gap between aspiration and action in George Eliot's heroines, and to the self-dramatisation it provokes, but her reading falls in too readily with the Middlemarch community assumption that women with a sense of their own potential are merely a nuisance. Even Elaine Showalter (1977), alert as she is to historical context, gives most of her attention to George Eliot's oppressiveness as a model for other nineteenth-century women writers, such as Mrs Oliphant, and assesses *The Mill on the Floss* as more acquiescent than the Brontës because it ends with the death of its heroine. Nina Auerbach's recent *Woman and the Demon* (1982), in contrast, emphasises the recalcitrant and the witch-like in Maggie, and her resistance to her society. In 'The Greening of Sister George' (1980) Showalter has since wittily traced the process of reconciliation visible in writing on George Eliot, and argues the case for her specific values as sister as well as writer.

## II

Theories of literature which result in blame for the most creatively achieving of women will raise questions about their own sufficiency—though we should also ask questions with a contrary bias about the adequacy of the criteria according to which we judge works of literature. Is the high place accorded to Jane Austen, George Eliot, Virginia Woolf, a result of their capitulation to encoded orthodoxies? Are they canonised as martyrs, and if so, in whose cause did their martyrdom occur? Such questions are raised by the series title of this book, which implies that the writers studied have a key place in the canon of literature which is specified by their occupying it as women writers.

The dangers of such 'genetic' reading are discussed in Peggy Kamuf's essay 'Writing Like a Woman'. She objects to understanding 'female writing' as 'works signed by biologically determined females of the species'. She warns of the 'temptation to explain to ourselves artistic and intellectual productions as expressions, simple and direct, of individual experience . . . such "feminist practice" must be prepared to ally itself with the fundamental assumptions of patriarchy which relies on the same principles' (McConnel-Ginet, 1980, p.286).

No neat or full equivalence, certainly, is possible between heterodoxy of lifestyle and of art. Those who live most at odds with the presumptions of their culture may engross their courage in that enterprise and avoid other forms of creative confrontation. It would be possible to read the relationship between George Eliot's life and work in this style: Mary Ann Evans, the rebel against her father's religious views; Marian Evans, the free-thinking and free-living literary journalist, the independent woman who had friendships with widely various men; Marian Lewes, Polly, Madonna, the lover of a married man who shared a life with him until his death and then married a man almost twenty years her junior,—yet the judiciously conservative writer, George Eliot. Such an account of the life, however, may serve the prejudices from which she freed herself. Her life required courage, independence and endurance, but the wish merely to flout society formed little part of it. The naming of her relationship with Lewes provides an example of the way in which we may mistakenly in retrospect read assertion as compliance.

Because they were not legally married to each other, George Eliot and George Lewes's relationship as husband and wife involved a constant and sustained commitment of themselves at a level less quiescent than that without marriage. To call each other 'husband' and 'wife' involved both assertion and reassertion. The need for continuous rededication gave a particular declarativeness to their relationship and endowed it with some of the yearning intensity of adultery as well as the security of marriage. This enriching doubleness was matched by privations—they were visited by rather few women and their gradual move towards acceptance in the intellectual visiting world retained a quality of paradox.

The persistent acts of choice against the odds, which are part of any love relationship outside marriage and give it a particular poignancy, may well have nourished both George Lewes and George Eliot creatively by keeping them always alert to feeling, and to contradiction and anomaly. At the same time the connubial solidity of their relationship was a radical challenge to society. They would not accept a peripheral, temporary or secret status for a love which was not ratified by law. We would be quite mistaken to see their claim of 'respectability' as merely acquiescence: it subverted the distinctions between 'pure' and 'impure', public and private, madonna and whore. George Eliot and Marian Lewes saw all those easy contraries as the enemy of a life truly lived. As she wrote to Barbara Bodichon: 'I am a very blessed woman, am I not? to have all this reason for being glad that I have lived; in spite of my sins and sorrows—or rather, by reason of my sins and sorrows.' Nina Auerbach remarks 'the fitful, rudderless, and self-doubting first half [of her life] was alchemized into gold when the austere bluestocking became the fallen woman.' (Auerbach, 1982, p.183). Lynn Linton's malicious and vigorous attack on George Eliot's achieved character, 'a made woman', expressed the contradictions in which George Eliot found herself. She wished, Linton wrote, 'to be at once conventional and insurgent . . . the self-reliant law-breaker and the eager postulant for the recognition granted only to the convenanted' (Linton, 1899; pp.97–8). She sustained relationships and acted out a life as little as possible bounded by society's curtailing demands. Yet her method was not one of zealous confrontation but of persistence. The style of her rebellion, such as it was, is represented in her decision to claim the name of Mrs Lewes, to insist on recognition in the terms understood by her society, of a relationship which transgressed its assumptions. She did not seek to conceal that 'transgression'. She challenged the name given to relationships—and challenged, too, the insistence on secrecy and the private which burdens love relationships outside marriage. The cost of such obduracy was high. It resulted in that formal claiming of exceptionalness, of the vatic and sibylline.

But writing, with its inevitable silence and sequestration, its intimate yet generalised claims on the reader, precisely expressed the course she had chosen. And fiction, with its exploration of consequences, possibilities, its pursuit of paths eschewed in life, gave her further lives to pursue. Moreover, the novelist is necessarily both law-breaker and law-giver, sympathising with those whose lives are chequered by law, yet re-weighting chance by the activity of writing narrative.

The often remarked fact that George Eliot wrote no fiction before she and Lewes lived together has many modes of explanation. Certainly his sustained encouragement gave her confidence without the fear of falling into an abyss of lovelessness. The process of writing, for George Eliot, demanded the same opening of the self, the same stirring of otherwise unshared memories, as the process of loving and therefore shared many of the same risks. The movement can be tracked in the ontological wooing of the reader by means of a narrative discourse which implies a speaking voice, silenced, except in imagination, but insistent.

The intellectual and emotional expansion created by accord and connection was of as much, or even more, value to her than was debate and confrontation. The extraordinary range of extending interests that Lewes and George Eliot shared supported her creativity. But there was another factor in their situation which made writing, with its brooding extension of silent insight, particularly apt. She lived a muted life, in which others needed to come to her not she to them (fearing as she did rebuffs and unwilling to submit herself to them). She shut her ears to criticism in order to sustain her creativity. She also lived a life of startling intellectual range and freedom, as her novels and her notebooks make clear. Deafness and sound are two poles of a long and crucial continuum in her metaphoric life. The silent urgency of a style which implies speech; the insistence on *voice*, dramatised in those recurrent women singers who form the type of the woman artist in her work; her reluctance to speak out directly on issues of the day lest her support do harm to causes she espoused; all these express the extent to which silent writing and reading gave dramatic expression to her particular psychic position. But not only to her own position. She seems both to have needed and to have feared her exceptionalness. Very late in life she remembered the wounds caused to her in her youth because other women thought her 'uncanny', witch-like in her possession of occult learning and powers, and thereby, equally, excluded, made peripheral to the everyday. She insists in her work on the *typicality* of her heroines' predicaments. And in her own activity of writing she incorporated the muting of women's voices, she dramatised the private, and dwelt in the unachieving, even while the scope of her fiction reclaimed the broadest extent of social inquiry and of critical insight into the workings of class, gender, age, power and need.

Her courage was silent. It took the form of writing, of private action, not of public campaign. In writing she can tease out the meaning of action with a profound but unyielding compunction. The intransigence of this insight perhaps helps to account for her knowledge of remorse. In her life, she made extreme, irrevocable commitments without confiding in her friends before-hand or insisting that they sympathise afterwards. Her moral fascination with renunciation went alongside a passionate grasp of what was possible. What to give up and what persistently to claim was the key problem for her.

What needed to be claimed by women when George Eliot began to write was not difference, which was taken for granted and used to circumscribe women, but likeness: likeness of capacity, of intellectual range, of emotional force and endurance, above all, likeness of *access* before real difference could be discovered.

> Let the whole field of reality be laid open to woman as well as to man, and then that which is peculiar to her mental modification, instead of being, as it is now, a source of discord and repulsion between the sexes, will be found to be a necessary complement to the truth and beauty of life. (Pinney, 1963, p.81)

So she wrote in 1854 in the typically optimistic formulation of her earliest journalism.

In the following year, she wrote an essay on 'Margaret Fuller and Mary Wollstonecraft' in which she quotes Margaret Fuller, approving her demonstration of 'the folly of absolute definitions of woman's nature and absolute demarcations of woman's mission'. 'Nature', George Eliot quotes from Fuller, 'seems to delight in varying the arrangements, as if to show that she will be fettered by no rule; and we must admit the same varieties that she admits' (ibid., p.203). Sixteen years later, she opens *Middlemarch* with an ironic glance at the false scientism of 'absolute definitions' of women's nature and 'absolute demarcations' of women's func-tions. John Stuart Mill in *The Subjection of Women* (1869)

11

also saw the circularity of descriptions of women's capacities which were based on their current curtailed role in society.

The likeness claimed is not identity, but rather the right to discovery and change: 'We want freedom and culture for woman, because subjection and ignorance have debased her, and with her, Man' (ibid., p.205). Cixous sees the couple man/woman as the underpinning opposition of language, but as *'hierarchized* opposition: superior/inferior' (Marks and Courtivron, 1981; Cixous, 1975). Moreover, Cixous asserts, in philosophy the 'absolute constant' is the opposition 'activity/passivity' which, traditionally, is coupled with sexual difference: 'in philosophy, woman is always on the side of passivity. Every time the question comes up: when we examine kinship structures; whenever a family model is brought into play; in fact as soon as the ontological question is raised' (Marks and Courtivron, 1981, p.91).

This question of how far women must be identified with passivity beset George Eliot throughout her career as a writer. From Comte she drew the formulation, appropriate both to men and women, that 'notre vie se compose de resignation et d'activité'. But she persistently questions, while never entirely escaping, the strong connection society has made between women and passivity. The intransigence of Antigone, with its special emphasis on resistance as activity, was one end of a heroic spectrum for her. The other was the passivity of the Madonna, accepting the special fate which is to set her apart from the ordinary lot of women, fulfilled by another's will. In both cases, separateness is emphasised. It is the *exceptionalness* as much as the typicality of the Virgin's fate as woman which fascinates her.

This small picture of Titian's [The Annunciation], . . . brought a new train of thought. It occurred to me that here was a great dramatic motive of the same class as those used by the Greek dramatists, yet specifically differing from them. A young maiden, believing herself to be on the eve of the chief event of her life—marriage—about to share in the ordinary lot of womanhood, full of young hope, has suddenly announced to her that she is chosen to fulfil a great destiny, entailing a terribly different experience from that of ordinary womanhood. (Haight, 1978, p.376)

In her notebooks we find frequent extracts which imply doubts about the extent to which men and women are different in nature, rather than in their upbringing in culture: 'The virtue of a man & of a woman is one & the same, says Plutarch' (Pratt and Neufeldt 1979; p.55); 'The Eagle were very unnatural if because she is able to do it, she should perch the whole day upon a tree, staring in contemplation of the majesty & glory of the sun, & let her young Eaglets starve in the nest" (Dr Donne, Letter to Sir H. Goodyere; ibid., p.63). The powers of women as members of the human species are, in that quotation, opposed to their duties of childbearing and rearing, their 'natural role'. The eagle is capable of looking at the sun, but as female eagle, must rather feed her children.

Reading Shakespeare's sonnets, she notes that 'Some of the sonnets are painfully abject. He adopts language which might be taken to describe the miserable slavery of oppressed wives: for example,

> "I am to wait, though waiting so be hell
> Nor blame your pleasure be it ill or well".'
> (Ibid., p.211)

# III

George Eliot's key topic is relations between women and men, men and women. These may be the relations between lovers, between wives and husbands, fathers and daughters, brothers and sisters, mothers and sons. Relationships between men and men, and between women and women, take their place in her novels, but the key bond is that between the sexes, with its immense power to yoke unlike people and to bind them in desire, or into flesh in generation. This contradiction—difference and connection—sustains the tension of her work. As Judith Wilt remarks, ' "yokelessness" is one of the worst ills that can befall a person in her fiction' (Wilt, 1980, p.206). She values interdependence even above independence: and she gives it that high valuation because of (as well as in spite of) its difficulty. The threats and burdens of connection are given as much meaning as its joys. Indeed, only rarely (as when Will and Dorothea at last kiss, letting slip all the hampering conditions which have kept them apart) is the rapture of connection shown.

In her narrative, the twinned insistence on difference and connection makes for a formidable complexity. Difference does not dissolve connection: connection does not do away with difference.

The insistence on these contradictory elements of experience, of narrative, and of language, does not, however, lead her to rest in dialectic, or dualism. Instead, it nurtures her power of sustained complexity. Her consciousness of the problems of traversing and of multiformity are shown in quotations such as that from Victor Hugo: 'L'inconvénient des mots, c'est d'avoir plus de contour que les idées. Toutes les idées se mêlent par les bords; les mots, non' (Pratt and Neufeldt, 1979, pp.

19-20); and from the *Rig-Veda*: 'Wise poets make the beautiful-winged, though he is one, manifold by words' (quoted ibid., p.221). Sometimes George Eliot expects structure to express too much, independent of content; sometimes, the complexity slackens into evasion, as Barbara Hardy and Geoffrey Hill have both remarked in different terms of *Felix Holt*. But her feeling for the urgency and difficulty of connection presses her narrative out into multiformity. And multiformity frees her from the drive back to origins, or on to resolution, which is implicit in polarised opposition.

I have described in an earlier book, *Darwin's Plots* (1983), the ways in which she registered evolutionary patterns of narrative in her work, and the extent to which she challenged any straightforwardly 'progressive' reading of Darwin. Imaginatively, she was attracted by the 'inextricable web of affinities' which Darwin saw as the order of physical life, and she grasped the emphasis on the individual case and on problems of categorisation which his work brought to the fore. I have suggested that she both learnt from and resisted the implications of his theories, particularly as they bore upon women's cultural and sexual roles. In the present study, I want to concentrate on other issues. But by whatever route we approach her writing, we shall find, always, a feeling for interconnection and yet a strong awareness of how difficult it is to keep different experiences simultaneously within meaning.

Her late books demonstrate how hard it is to make stories stay connected, an awareness which supplements her earlier emphasis on how hard it is to keep them apart. Both pulls are figured in the relations between men and women, though they are not exclusively concerned with those relations.

Cixous goes on to suggest, in the passage I have earlier

discussed, that 'as soon as there is a will to say something
. . . you are led right back—to the father' (Marks and
Courtivron, 1981, p.91) As we shall see, the struggle to
write in, and then to write out, the father, is significant
for George Eliot's creative enterprise. She works at the
problem at the level of plot and characterisation and in
the blanching out of the male narrator in her later
works. Without 'writing in milk' she both incorporates
and goes beyond the male persona, transforming and
extending him into her own image as a human scribe
who is, historically, woman. But the mother, also,
becomes a disturbing figure for her. In her 1857 review
of *Aurora Leigh* she says that Elizabeth Barrett Browning
'has shown herself all the greater poet because she is
intensely a poetess', (*The Westminster Review*, 67, 1857,
p.306) one who *'superadds'* to the masculine 'all the
peculiar powers without the negations of her sex'. But,
alongside her analysis in the review of the characteristic
strengths of the woman writing, who can include and go
on beyond the masculine, she insists that liberty in
sexual identity gives liberty *from* sexual type: 'there is
simply a full mind pouring itself out in song as its natural
and easiest medium.' (That image of the singer will recur
in her symbolic system.)

Childbearing distinguishes women from men but
need not define woman. The metaphors of womb and
milk that Kristeva and Cixous employ, though full of
comfort and recognition, risk being read as biological
determinism. They may function to fix the idea of the
woman writing as essentially reproductive. So, while
respecting difference, we should be wary of the
imprimatur of our generative organs as a sufficient
description of creativity. Writing as a woman must
mean writing as a human. George Eliot's writing
emphasises universals. As Kamuf remarks:

Western culture has . . . traditionally reserved a special category for the intellectual or cultural production of women, intimating their special status as exceptions within those realms where 'to think male thoughts' is not to be distinguished from thinking in universals. (McConnell-Ginet, 1980, p.285)

Or as Nina Auerbach reminds us, in the period when George Eliot was writing:

Women were seen as by nature deficient in the capacity for abstraction; even John Stuart Mill's radical *The Subjection of Women* concedes that women's bent may be for 'the practical' rather than for 'general principles'. (Auerbach, 1982, pp.54–5)

This may explain why many who hear a woman's voice in Jane Austen's writing, do not do so in George Eliot's. Her writing as a woman takes the full measure of human experience.

# IV

George Eliot thought it important not to idealise women as they currently exist. Using the metaphor that occurs over and over again in feminist writing of this period, she turns to the analogy with slavery. It was an important metaphor because of its topicality, because the history of the slaves in America had already made it clear that change is possible and that enfranchisement is a real political event, and because it allowed an analysis of the psychological effects of enslavement. Here George Eliot makes it clear that we should not be too ready to claim superiority for the enslaved lest it appear that slavery produces moral advantages:

17

Unfortunately, many over-zealous champions of women assert their actual equality with men—nay, even their moral superiority to men—as a ground for their release from oppressive laws and restrictions. They lose strength immensely by this false position. If it were true, then there would be a case in which slavery and ignorance nourished virtue, and so far we should have an argument for the continuance of bondage. (Pinney, 1963, p.205)

These views may help us more exactly pose our reading of George Eliot's women characters. The danger of the Margaret Fuller/Marian Evans argument is that it may become a form of blaming women, as an antidote to idealising them. Critique may become costive. This gives a specific value to *sympathy*. The observing (and therefore privileged) woman writer must move through analysis and critique to *feel with* the women observed, sustaining the bond of likeness. Such a position, in which sympathy disclaims privilege, also gives a particular value to *feeling with men* on the part of the observing woman. It registers her freedom and enlarges her range of access to human experience, certainly. It acknowledges gender but looses its containment. At the same time it is a form of claim, a claim to knowledge and to free likeness, even while it is more apparently a form of self-abnegation. Writing of men with the same sympathetic completeness as of women is an effortless representation of women's scope and authority in George Eliot's writing.

It is less readily granted that women writers can convincingly characterise men than that men can characterise women. Leslie Stephen attacked George Eliot on these grounds. Implicitly it is assumed that manhood, being larger in scope, includes understanding of women, while lesser women must strain to encompass men's wider lives. Henry James, however, while demurring at Will Ladislaw as 'a woman's man', yet saw how male writers' descriptions of women have 'an indefinable appeal to masculine prejudice—to a sort of titillation of the masculine sense of difference', whereas George Eliot's description of women and of men 'is more philosophic—more broadly intelligent' (Carroll, 1971, pp.356-7). Generalisation, under the pen of Bacon, La Rochefoucauld, even Pascal, codifies and imprints. It contains truth, rather than liberating it. This constraining force in the maxim is very different from George Eliot's use of generalisation. Generalisation in her work draws in the reader, yokes diversity in unexpected kinship, but emphasises equally the extended human community:

> Because her voice sympathetically articulates opposed perspectives, because it is highly provisional and tentative even as it risks generalisations, this narrator becomes an authentic 'we', a voice of the community that is committed to accepting the indeterminacy of meaning, as well as the complex kinship of people and things. (Gilbert and Gubar, 1979, p.253)

George Eliot wrote of the maxims of La Rochefoucauld as being like 'the vase which the action of fire has made light, brittle and transparent' (Pinney, 1963, p.74). The hard brilliance and fragility of curtailed truth has little resemblance to George Eliot's method. Indeed, she demurs at the constriction of human possibility in La Rochefoucauld's observations. They are

> at once undeniably true and miserably false; true as applied to that condition of human nature in which the selfish instincts are still dominant, false if taken as a representation of all the elements and possibilities of human nature. (Ibid., p.75)

Her mode of generalisation realises the 'possibilities of human nature' as well as sharply epitomising curtailment in human action. The difference between the two modes may be said to be that between con-forming and dis-covering.

In her work, generalisation is more often concerned with making connections than with establishing limits. Its mode is imagistic. It recreates in our activity of mind the making of connection, so that we are led to assess our relationship, uneasy and according, to what is described. Her generalised ideal figures, such as Antigone, are both specifically female and capable of standing for the full range of human difficulty.

Why, then, did George Eliot adopt a male pseudonym? Like Currer Bell (Charlotte Brontë) she might wish to avoid the condescension of male critics towards female writers. But as G.H. Lewes had pointed out in 'The Lady Novelists' in *The Westminster Review* (58, 1852, pp. 129–41), many of the finest novelists of the past fifty years and the present day were women. He heads his article with the names of George Sand, Miss Austen, Mrs Gore, Mrs Marsh, Mrs Trollope, Miss Jewsbury, Currer Bell and Mrs Gaskell. Only one of these, you will observe, is writing under a man's name and that for a novel describing in first person the life of a woman. Later in the same article Lewes says that *Jane Eyre*

> was not only attributed to a man, but one of the most keen witted and observing of female writers dogmatically pronounced upon internal evidence that none but a man could have written it. (p.139)

The grounds of this opinion were its 'force and fierceness'. By the time George Eliot, four years later, comments on women writers of novels in 'Silly Novels by

Lady Novelists', she observes that respected women writers are treated on the same terms with men, and only the untalented are given special quarter. Writing in the guise of a consciously male persona herself, she attempts to divest 'the mere fact of feminine authorship' from any 'false prestige which may give it a delusive attraction'. Insisting on her own 'plainness of speech' in opposition to 'the choicest phraseology of puffery' by which lady authors are commonly greeted, she points out:

> No sooner does a woman show that she has genius or effective talent, than she receives the tribute of being moderately praised and severely criticised . . . Harriet Martineau, Currer Bell, and Mrs Gaskell have been treated as cavalierly as if they had been men. And every critic who forms a high estimate of the share women may ultimately take in literature, will, on principle, abstain from any exceptional indulgence towards the productions of literary women. (Pinney 1963; p.322)

So, the fear of condescension will not on its own explain her use of persona.

A more persuasive cause is that she has already created a body of intellectual work in her journalism that she chooses to exempt from the new and risky creative venture of novel writing. If George Eliot fails, Marian Evans remains intact. That reason would be more complete were it not the case that all her journalism was published anonymously, and her identity was known only within an immediate literary circle. Still, that *was* her circle, and she might well choose not to put her reputation at risk within it.

More urgent yet, was the fear that people would not be able to read or listen to her text if they were to identify it with the free-living intellectual woman, so recently become the unmarried companion of George Henry Lewes. That reason was compelling, certainly, and it was a literary as well as a sociological reason for anonymity. 'George Eliot' was name without person. It emptied her text of context, making it speak within the terms of its own statements and representations. However, the space was not quite cleansed of association. The chosen name was emphatically a man's, though there is a witty sub-text of George Eliot's own celebratory devising. George is both George Lewes's first name, and the first half of the pseudonym, George Sand (Thomson, 1977, p.158).

Eliot, who knows? It shares initial and number of letters with Evans; it is the name Jane Eyre adopted in her solitary wanderings, and, if we are to believe Ruby Redinger, which I do not, it signifies an indirect tribute to Lewes: to Lewes I O It.

She liked the name. She leaves parental authority. She 'makes a name for herself'. She chooses her own patronymic. For the time being, she casts the 'author' as a male origin for the text. According to a recent male commentator (if names are to be believed) Michael P. Ginsburg (1980, p.546):

Writing is the process by which a woman—Mary Ann Evans—becomes a man—George Eliot. Writing, the most common metaphor for which is weaving, is the symbolic way by which a woman produces herself a phallus.

Well, Eliot spelt backwards is 'toile'—woven fabric, an oddity which Ginsburg has not observed. Certainly, weaving is an important metaphor in her work, as Gilbert and Gubar have pointed out (1979, pp.519-28), and it is an activity on which I shall comment later. For the time being, though, note simply the phallocentric assumption that the woman writing is rewarded with a handwoven phallus (a useless object if ever there was one). Ginsburg fails to remark that her subsequent fame unravels the phallus and reworks the name George Eliot into the form of the woman's body, the woman writing. Ginsburg draws (presumably) here on Freud's essay on 'Femininity' in which Freud remarks that:

> it seems that women have made few contributions to the discoveries and inventions in the history of civilisation; there is, however, one technique which they may have invented—that of plaiting and weaving. If that is so, we should be tempted to guess the unconscious motive for the achievement. Nature herself would seem to have given the model which this achievement imitates by causing the growth at maturity of the pubic hair that conceals the genitals. The step that remained to be taken lay in making the threads adhere to one another, while on the body they stick into the skin and are only matted together. If you reject this idea as fantastic and regard my belief in the influence of lack of penis on the configuration of femininity as an *ideé fixe*, I am of course defenceless. (Freud, 1971, p.596)

Freud is here defenceless. He and George Eliot both draw on a shared, and complex, metaphor, which is everywhere in Victorian writing: the web (Beer, 1983, pp.149–80). But she avoids naturalising weaving as women's work. Silas Marner, in an historically more correct attribution of labour division, is a weaver (and becomes both foster-mother and father). In *Daniel Deronda*, George Eliot actually contrasts free creativity and the woman's work of spinning and weaving in her allusion to Erinna, the young woman poet who in Ancient Greek legend died frustrated, chained by her mother to the spinning-wheel (Paris, 1959, pp.539–58).

But her use of male pseudonym problematises the way

we should refer to narrative discourse in her work. Some critics, demonstrating that they do not innocently confuse source and writing, use the masculine form, as Knoepflmacher (1968) does. This is a perfectly honourable, but not entirely satisfactory, solution. I shall use the female form throughout this study since for much of her life as a novelist the name 'George Eliot' signified a female origin. For similar reasons, I shall retain the name she chose for herself, 'George Eliot', and not convert it back again into a pseudo-patronymic, 'Eliot'.

George Eliot ceased to be Mary Ann or Marian Evans before she became George Eliot (a name by which she was never addressed). She claimed the name of Marian Lewes, and claimed it as a badge of acknowledgement, not of subservience. Her claims that their relationship be respected and open were radical ones, founded on 'mutual faithfulness and mutual devotion' (Simcox *Autobiography*: Bodley MS., p.126) and not at all on law.

She never permitted to any of the women in her fiction such radical acts as she herself took, except perhaps to the Princess Halm-Eberstein, in her last novel, Deronda's mother, the great singer Alchirisi, who has given away her child to devote herself to the freedom of her career. The plot of *Daniel Deronda* turns on her need to mortify herself, to knit up again the unyielding continuities of descent and culture, but not, let it be noted, to renege on her choice. She has no wish to re-establish the mothering relationship with Deronda, but she feels compelled to re-endow him with the longer birthright of his Jewishness. She half-hopes that he will repudiate those claims, but he does not. George Eliot eschewed motherhood, and had to learn to control and move outside a mothering metaphor in her relationship to the characters within her fiction. Stepmothers are notably absent from her fiction—notably, because that was the role she took on in life towards Lewes's three sons, one of whom she nursed devotedly through his last illness.

One goal of writing may be the escape from gender, and it would be a mistake to loop all imaginative writing back into the ghetto of gender, what the Marxist-Feminist Collective describes as criticism that subsumes 'the text into the sexually-defined personality of its author, and thereby obliterates its literarity' (Vol. 3, 1978, p.31). But though the arc of desire may be escape from gender, the pre-conditions of the writing are bound to the writer's experience as social, sexual, historical being and the writing itself is a part of its culture. In the case of George Eliot we have a striking example of a writer who sought to slough off the contextuality of her own name and enter a neutral space for her writing.

That is an abstract and an idealised description of a process which cost much. It cost much because it brought with it deceit and secrecy, the possibility of betraying what she sought to sustain, of a too easy alliance with power. George Eliot's first critics, at the time of the publication of *Scenes of Clerical Life* and *Adam Bede*, could at once characterise the writer. He was clearly male, probably young, and almost certainly a clergyman; though his exact place on the spectrum of religious opinion was held to be uncertain because of his perhaps over-capacious sympathies. Once the news was out that George Eliot was a woman, Marian Evans, intellectual journalist and consort of G.H. Lewes, the critics forthwith described her feminine qualities as a writer, her excellence in details, her incapacity for large-scale invention, her tendency to feminise her men and idealise her heroines.

It is a salutary story. But the story does not end there.

# George Eliot

George Eliot became a brooding presence, 'man-womanly and woman-manly' as Virginia Woolf's persona in *A Room of One's Own* said true writers must be. It became less easy as George Eliot's career progressed to see her simply as a reconciliation or opposition of known poles, 'a man's intellect and a woman's heart', which was the first attempt to domesticate her writing or exculpate her behaviour. 'She had organically, all the (str) intellectual strength of a man and (all) in feeling all the peculiar weaknesses of woman' (Haight, 1978, VIII, p.131). So another solution was chosen. She was 'a sibyl': woman as prophet, amazingly learned, exceptional, peripheral, powerful but inactive. In an early project, which was never written, George Eliot suggested a companion-piece for her 'Woman in France', to be called 'Woman in Germany' in which in 'the earliest historic twilight . . . its women were prophetesses' (Haight, 1954, II, p.190). At the roots of development she suggests, is woman's prophetic role. In her own life, so far as it was public, she seems in later years to have accepted the characterisation of herself as sibylline. The role emphasised disengagement. It exempted her from being a part of the world of genetic descent (it freed her from the actuality and the metaphor of motherhood). It gave a more than social meaning to the activity of generalisation, while avoiding religious claims.

The metaphor of 'sibyl' had another function. It emphasised that she was *exceptional*, both anomalous and distinguished. This aspect was, perhaps unconsciously, welcome to the admiring men by whom she was surrounded. Her case did not make it necessary to rethink the situation of all women. She could become genius or freak rather than a representative of the capacities of other, equal, less-known women. Her sequestration made her assimilable back into society as it stood, not bringing about general change but voicing vatic insights which enforced no action. That was how her most unsympathetic critics, such as Lynn Linton, saw her position.

Yet such criticism is telling, I believe, in relation to her life not her writing. And though the life of a great writer has a meaning which cannot be ignored, it should not be made identical with what is written. Far from it. The distinction between life and writing has a particular force in the case of women writers, whose lives in the past may have been essentially means of surviving curtailment with dignity, while in their writing they find issue out of curtailment.

'Mighty is the power of motherhood', the narrator quotes in George Eliot's first published fiction, *Scenes of Clerical Life*. As her work goes on she brings that power and its significance under more and more complicated scrutiny both at the level of characterisation and of narrative order. Giving birth releases energies which shake the present order. Incipience and revolution are implicit in the childbearing metaphor as well as nurturing and conserving (*Spanish Gypsy*, p.8):

> 'Feeding an embryo Future, offspring strange
> Of the fond Present, that with mother-prayers
> And mother-fancies looks for championship
> Of all her loved beliefs and old-world ways
> From that young Time she bears within her womb'.

Mothering was a powerful metaphor for her, and one she had to learn first to control and then to dissolve in her relationship to the fictions that she created.

In her later books she brought into question that identification of the father, the law, and the origin, which still preoccupies psychoanalytic theory through the long inheritance of Freud and the new reading of Lacan. One line of argument issuing from that identification is represented in Jane Gallop's *Feminism and Psychoanalysis: The Daughter's Seduction* (1982), which argues that because the paternal law (in this case, psychoanalysis) is constituted arbitrarily through the appropriation of language, language itself must be seduced. Feminism must undermine the categories of language. The male/female distinction must be shown to be arbitrary (Gallop, 1982, p.58). George Eliot participates in the undermining of polarities. Her persistent use of 'we' is not so much liberal as stringent, binding us across categories and collapsing privileged distance. The 'we' of her text moves, often with deliberate disturbance, askance gender, class, and time. Sometimes the solidarity of 'we' is comforting, suggesting identity of desire and values. As often, it is discomfiting. It embarrasses because it destabilises categories. George Eliot's facetiousness is often an indication that such a point of difficulty has been reached, and she then sometimes uses 'we' as refuge. 'We' can express community and complicity. It is a form which denies polarisation. It includes a moving population. George Eliot never uses it to the reader in the intimate and exclusive form of lovers—two only participating in the 'we', though we may at times almost believe so. There are always other unknown human beings included, as well as the writer writing and the known figures of the characters in the fiction.

But the erotic force of 'we' is not entirely absent. The reader is wooed into intimacy by its recurrence. And it is a form which sustains the writing ontologically as much as it does the reading. The observations within the writing are freed from circumscription, endowed with large as well as enigmatic meaning. The reader of these fictions feels chosen, and the wooing and choosing are not held within the male/female polarity. The writing allows us, through passionate inhabiting of diversity, to move outside the prescriptions of gender-roles with which, however various, we enter. It gives us intelligence.

The reader will have noted how many of the terms we habitually use to describe what determines us derive from what is written: *'circumscribed'* and *'prescription'*, are two that have occurred here: and how 'intelligence' bears the sense of message and of secret—as well as of the capacity to interpret messages. The writer is well placed to test these categories and limits inscribed as law. George Eliot does that by a method which challenges essentialism by *inclusion*.

Chapter Two

# Marian Evans:
# Reading Women Writers

*I*

In the mid-1850s, before she began to write fiction and took on the pseudonym George Eliot, Marian Evans was already an established translator, literary journalist and editor. All Victorian journalism at that time was published anonymously, so that the power of her contribution to the *Westminster Review*, though well known to an inner circle of acquaintances, would have been invisible to the outside world. Moreover, even that circle of acquaintances did not know, unless they happened to be told, which articles were by which writer. The Wellesley Index makes it possible for us now to have a far more analytical understanding of Victorian journals than was possible to contemporaries, to whom the common voice of the journal would have been overridingly important. The *Westminster Review*, of which George Eliot was the assistant editor, was a liberal intellectual journal occupied with a broad range of issues of the day, not only with literature or with politics, but with such developing fields as anthropology, evolutionary theory, and sociology. Like most other journals of the time, it was largely written by men and addressed to men. George Eliot seems to have welcomed the anonymity which gave her the freedom to range with authority. Writing to Charles Bray, for example, two weeks after the appearance of her trenchant and scholarly article attacking Dr Cumming for the 'unscrupulosity' of his theological writing (writing which claimed to interpret Biblical prophecy and myth in a style which she describes as 'slippery and lax') she wryly says: 'The article appears to have produced a strong impression, and that impression would be a little counteracted if the author were known to be a *woman*' (Haight, 1954, II, p.218). It would be counteracted particularly, it seems, because the intellectual grasp displayed by the writing cuts across stereotypes. Its analytical authority would be reinterpreted as female captiousness.

With a nice irony, her formidable essay is immediately preceded in the same issue of the *Westminster Review* by John Chapman's long article on 'The Position of Women in Barbarism and Among the Ancients', in part a review of Lady Morgan's *Woman and Her Master*. Chapman points to the very different interpretations of the past we gain from the evidence of law and romances: law shows woman to be oppressed, romances suggest that she is accorded the highest value. Chapman argues across this contradiction that women, whether demeaned or worshipped, have been essentially treated as property throughout the ages, and that their position has been identified with that of slaves. Indeed he argues as Engels would thirty years later in 1884 in *The Origin of the Family, Private Property and the State* that 'the existence of slavery side by side with monogamy . . . stamps monogamy from the very beginning with its specific character of monogamy *for the woman only'* (Engels, 1972, p.126), Chapman writes: 'Unable to comply with its provisions, they annul it as regards themselves, but enforce it with frightful severity on their frailer companions (*Westminster Review*, 64, 1855, p.383).

Chapman's discussion of the double standard leads into an analysis of laws as they bear on women; he points out that the laws of England have not yet reached the degree of enlightenment of the Romans. He concludes:

> We must remember that it is *in spite* of English laws that English women have now virtually attained a degree of social freedom and dignity worthy of comparison with that of their Roman predecessors. (Ibid., p.435)

At around this time also, John Chapman had turned his amatory attention away from Marian Evans, under pressure from his wife and his lover. George Eliot copied into her Commonplace Book the following from Guizot's *Histoire*:

> Partout la pensée morale des hommes s'élève et aspire fort au dessus de leur vie. Et gardez-vous de croire que parce qu'elle ne gouvernait pas immédiatement les actions, parce que la pratique démentait sans cesse et étrangement la théorie, l'influence de la théorie fut nulle et sans valeur.

## II

Although the *Westminster Review* was predominantly written by men it would be misleading to represent George Eliot as an entirely isolated and exceptional figure. Harriet Martineau, a frequent contributor, whose contributions range across philosophy, politics and history, was already well established. (George Eliot in 1852 wrote that she is 'the only English woman that possesses thoroughly the art of writing' (Haight, 1954, II, p.32).) There were other, less familiar names: Jane Sinnett, who wrote the literature section in the early 1850s; and Caroline Frances Cornwallis who died in 1858 and who wrote two powerful articles: one, on the 'Capabilities and Disabilities of Women' appeared in 1857 (vol. 67, pp. 42–72) alongside Marian Evans's essay on 'Worldliness and Other-Worldliness: The Poet Young' (ibid., pp.1–42), and another, on 'The Property of Married Women' appeared in the previous year (vol. 66, pp.331–60) in the same issue as Evans's 'Silly Novels by Lady Novelists' (ibid., pp.442–61).

The collocation of Cornwallis and Evans emphasises an important point. Marian Evans did not write in any detail about the social conditions of women, though in her discussion of women writers such as Madame de Sablé she touched on their continuing social disabilities. She writes extensively on German literature, on philosophy and theology, and reviews a very wide range of works, including fiction. Her position at the time is well epitomised in the concluding paragraph of 'Woman in France; Madame de Sablé' in which she asserts that 'the superiority of womanly development' in seventeenth century France has 'an important bearing on the culture of women in the present day' (Pinney, 1963, p.80).

We have no faith in feminine *conversazioni*, where ladies are eloquent on Apollo and Mars; though we sympathize with the yearning activity of faculties which, deprived of their proper material, waste themselves in weaving fabrics out of cobwebs. (Ibid., 80-1)

She had, for herself, already escaped the debilitated education which left a gap between ostentation and yearning 'deprived of their proper materials'. *Proper* here bears a particular weight. Marian Evans never fell into the trap, still a real one both for her admirers and detractors, of believing that knowledge particularly and properly belonged to men. If aspiring women 'waste themselves in weaving fabrics out of cobwebs' this is not because they cannot weave well, but because they are denied access to more enduring yarns.

At this stage in her career, George Eliot is still under the sway of phrenology and of the belief in physique as determining brain power:

> What were the causes of this earlier development and more abundant manifestation of womanly intellect in France? The primary one, perhaps, lies in the physiological characteristics of the Gallic race: the small brain and vivacious temperament which permit the fragile system of woman to sustain the superlative activity requisite for intellectual creativeness; while, on the other hand, the larger brain and slower temperament of the English and Germans are, in the womanly organization, generally dreamy and passive. The type of humanity in the latter may be grander, but it requires a larger sum of conditions to produce a perfect specimen. (Ibid., p.55)

Perhaps we can hear her own self-doubts in her comments on slow English women. As Bessie Rayner Parkes wrote to Barbara Leigh Smith in March 1852:

> Large angels take a long time unfolding their wings; but when they do, soar out of sight. Miss Evans either has no wings, or, which I think is the case, they are coming, budding. (Haight, 1954, II, p.9)

In 'Woman in France', Marian Evans, in her anonymous

guise, suggests that the second permitting factor in women's achievement in France has been 'the laxity of opinion and practice with regard to the marriage-tie'.

> Gallantry and intrigue are sorry enough things in themselves, but they certainly serve better to arouse the dormant faculties of woman than embroidery and domestic drudgery.

[Moreover]

> unions formed in the maturity of thought and feeling, and grounded only on inherent fitness and mutual attraction, tended to bring women into more intelligent sympathy with men. (Pinney, 1963, p.56)

The essay was her first piece of writing after her elopement with Lewes and has, in our hindsight knowledge, clear personal application. But this was not so at the time, even among those who knew her well. Charles Bray and George Combe, the phrenologist, had an agitated correspondence about her action which Combe held would harm reform movements, particularly the 'cause of religious freedom'. In the midst of their discussion Bray praises 'Harriet Martineau's' article (in fact, George Eliot's) in the last *Westminster Review* on 'French Woman': 'It is very clever and contains the only true and just distinction between the sexes I have ever seen' (Haight 1978, VIII, p.127). What his view of the distinction can be is perhaps obscured rather than elucidated in his next letter to Combe commenting on the elopement, in which he significantly shifts tense to put her qualities in the past: 'I don't think she is *mad*. She had organically, all the intellectual strength of a man and in feeling all the peculiar weaknesses of woman' (Ibid., p.131).

The intellectual strength of 'a man' and the emotional weaknesses of 'woman'—this familiar polarisation beset George Eliot. She strove to find ways of collapsing it, though she was well aware of the restrictions of power experienced by even liberated women. Was she simply indulging in editorial shifting of blame when she earlier wrote to Combe?

> If I were sole editor of the Westminster, I would take the responsibility on myself, and ask you to send them through me, but being a woman and something less than half an editor, I do not see how the step you propose could be taken. (Ibid., p.90)

It is a masculine tradition which claims 'reason' as male, 'emotion' as female but many women—then and now—adopt it, and seek power by the means it allows. That was what Sarah Ellis recommended doing in *Woman's Mission*, and in discussing *Middlemarch* we shall later see George Eliot's response to such arguments. Ruby Redinger accepts another traditional opposition:

> As hers was an extraordinarily powerful nature, it is little wonder that for the many years during which she was caught between the need for and fear of both masculine aggressiveness and feminine passivity, her sense of identity was blunted. (Redinger, 1976, p.59)

Certainly, George Eliot saw women as experienced in emotion, necessarily attentive to the movements of affection in themselves and others. To excel, or even to survive, in the area designated theirs (the private relationship, the household and family) it was necessary to be so. Such skills were learned, and accumulated socially and historically, but they were not the only ones native to women.

Historically, women had been sequestered from education, yet George Eliot felt and knew her own intellectual powers: 'For her, too, the burden and complexity of womanhood were not enough; she must reach beyond the sanctuary and pluck for herself the strange, bright fruits of art and knowledge' (Woolf, 1925, p.217-8).

The judgement is correct, but the terms are too exotic. To George Eliot learning and reading were not strange so much as familiar, needed, at home. Others told her about women's intellectual incapacities. She did not experience them in herself; and in the figure of Maggie she showed the passionately creative experience of reading and learning as a woman.

Elizabeth Barrett Browning in her poem, 'To George Sand: A Desire' (1844), wished for 'the brain of a man and the heart of a woman'. Dinah Mulock alludes to that line in a review of *The Mill on the Floss*, ironically, since the tenor of that novel is precisely to undercut any such polarisation by means of its pictures of Tom and Maggie Tulliver. Mulock writes of George Eliot as the

> author who has pre-eminently what all novelists should have, 'the brain of a man and the heart of a woman', united with what we may call a sexless intelligence, clear and calm, able to observe, and reason, and guide mortal passions, as those may, who have come out of the turmoil of the flesh into the region of ministering spirits . . . What if the messenger testify falsely? (Carroll, 1976, p.158)

Mulock's arresting question refers to George Eliot's refusal to provide moral resolution at the end of the work, letting it remain a 'passionately written presentment of temptation never conquered'. George Eliot's refusal to offer models which will resolve dilemmas troubled George Eliot's Victorian readers (as it has done some of her modern ones, though the models sought differ). Her capacity for sustained puzzling over problems and personal relationships rarely offers satisfying ways out. The value of the characters' experience, indeed, is measured by the power to sustain puzzlement and to acknowledge passionate feeling. The value of the reader's experience is that of entering multiple irreconcilable passions through enabling analysis.

Intellectual opportunity is emotional opportunity for women in her work, but she argued that women should not model themselves on men, nor pit themselves against them. Nowhere does she imply, as Gilbert and Gubar suggest, that by intellectual malnourishment 'emotional life is ' . . . enriched for women' (Gilbert and Gubar, 1979, p.498).

In this early period of her writing we can see Marian Evans struggling with problems of equivocal discourse which will at first beset the narrative figure of George Eliot too. Anonymity liberates the writer, but it unsettles the relationship to the reader. It gives authority and removes the author. It emphasises condescension, as when she describes Bremer's humour as 'of that easy, domestic kind which throws a pleasant light on every-day things' (Pinney, 1963, p.331).

Many of her statements sound more radical now that we know she is a woman than when they were read as normatively male. She clearly enjoyed the subterfuge at times, facetiously emphasising her masculine qualities. But some remarks could achieve their ironic force only when she is known to be a female source of writing. Otherwise their condescension colludes in a low estimate of women's powers, as much as in a mild alerting of men's self-criticism. George Eliot's own fears and ambitions contribute to the mock-solemn tone of her address at that time to inadequate women writers. Much later in her life, she said that she had been

> too proud and ambitious to write: I did not believe that I could do anything fine, and I did not choose to do anything of that mediocre sort which I despised when it was done by others. I began, however, by a sort of writing which had no great glory belonging to it, but which I felt certain I could do faithfully and well. (Haight, 1978, VIII, p.384)

The early Marian Evans is analysing practically what she sees as characteristic of masculine poor style, as well as of feminine 'silly novels'. She is aware of the dangers of adopting writing models which don't fit:

> With a few remarkable exceptions, our feminine literature is made up of books which could have been better written by men ... when not a feeble imitation, then they are usually an absurd exaggeration of the masculine style, like the swaggering gait of a bad actress in male attire. (Pinney, 1963 p.53)

In *Scenes of Clerical Life* the narrator twice refers to his tail-coats and at times there are deliberately swashbuckling appropriations of male manners in the language of the early reviews and of the two books written while her pseudonym still held its secret, *Scenes* and *Adam Bede*. These serve to reinforce the 'masculine' provenance of the writing and playfully to dramatise that persona.

At the end of her review of *Hertha*, by the feminist Swedish novelist Fredrika Bremer, whose work she admired, she takes Bremer to task for associating women's fitness to study medicine, not with the hard drudgery of real practice, but with the vicissitudes of a love-story.

39

Women have not to prove that they can be emotional, and rhapsodic, and spiritualistic; every one believes that already. They have to prove that they are capable of accurate thought, severe study, and continuous self-command. (Ibid., 1963: 334)

She concludes her essay by quoting approvingly Hertha's complaint against 'the ignorance in which women are left of Natural Science': 'the want of knowledge, the want of opportunity to acquire it, has caused nature to be to me a sealed book.' Her own argument is that if women are to pursue knowledge and effective activity they must not be fobbed off with 'cloudy eloquence' but must receive grounded education.

At the end of 'Silly Novels by Lady Novelists' she sees the writing of fiction as both opportunity and delusive resource for women:

No educational restrictions can shut women out from the materials of fiction, and there is no species of art which is so free from rigid requirements. Like crystalline masses, it may take any form, and yet be beautiful; we have only to pour in the right elements—genuine observation, humour, and passion. But it is precisely this absence of rigid requirement which constitutes the fatal seduction of novel-writing to incompetent women. (Ibid., p.324)

This essay is unsisterly because of its writer's refusal to acknowledge that she also is female, beset by the problems of other women writers. She shields herself with a masculine *de haut en bas* tone. She is, as she says, 'too proud and ambitious to write'. Yet the quality of her analysis and the vehemence with which she attacks poor novels by women show the tantalised ambition to be mounting.

## IV

Later in her career, George Eliot found it harassing to read contemporary novels, and it was to Jane Austen that she returned for the measure of her art. We can find traces of her reading of Jane Austen throughout her career, as Ellen Moers has brilliantly shown in her comparison of *Adam Bede* and *Emma*, though she was temperamentally and artistically less at home with those plots of double meaning and intrigue in which Jane Austen excels. Second readings of Jane Austen free us from the tonic experience of misreading which we must initially undergo. We are embarrassed, and justified by our subsequent self-correction. No such complete correction is possible in reading George Eliot. She yokes widely diverse plots together, and turns to the grammar of melodrama to bring about large changes in her plots, agents such as Raffles and Rigg, floods and boating accidents. She is close to Jane Austen, though, in those scenes of silent and passionate reinterpretation of the past such as we find in the meditations of Elizabeth and Emma, Dorothea and Gwendolen. The unwilled lucidity of regret mounts through the record of consciousness: Gwendolen, who is an Emma *in extremis*, an Emma violated rather than humiliated, is described thus:

> The thought that is bound up with our passion is as penetrative as air—everything is porous to it; bows, smiles, conversation, repartee, are mere honeycombs where such thought rushes freely, not always with a taste of honey. (*Daniel Deronda* III, pp.87–8, ch.48)

It is in the representation of remorse, with its endless replay of the past, its obsessional search for fresh reading, a reading which will allow issue out of fixed scenes, that George Eliot draws most closely on the emotional artistry of Jane Austen.

Where Jane Austen's early art thrived on the upendings of pastiche, George Eliot refers fugitively to other texts, or at an angle which does not at first reveal them. She engages with the work of writers she respects, or is troubled by, by means of expansion, taking the implications of words and events where they have failed to go.

George Eliot's response to other women writing fiction in the 1850s shows her challenging assumptions through revision, opening up oversealed contradictions and pressing them apart. Throughout her career she manifested a desire to reconcile events and people, a desire outwitted by an equally obdurate sense of how far things hold apart. She refuses the idea of the 'blameless victim' and writes apropos Antigone, that 'we shall never be to able to attain a great right without also doing a wrong' (Pinney, 1963, p.264). Antigone's 'defiant hardness' reminds us that 'a man must not only dare to be right, he must also dare to be wrong—to shake faith, to wound friendship, perhaps, to hem in his own powers'. (Ibid., p.265). The female figure of Antigone includes men too, generating the human drive of 'reformers, martyrs, revolutionists'. George Eliot effortlessly takes the woman as the general figure containing within it the human dilemmas of men as well as women. This generalisation of the female figure of Antigone reaches a more powerful and confident feminist position than the particular needs that Gilbert and Gubar attribute to her attachment:

> Eliot was profoundly drawn to Antigone's revolt against the misogynist King Creon because it is motivated by loyalty to a brother, Polynices, and because it takes the form of a

rejection of marriage. (Gilbert and Gubar, 1979, p.494)

Antigone, like George Eliot, is a law-breaker with a profound respect for law and an obdurate capacity to resist its claims. Taking risks, daring to shake, to wound, to fail, are essential to George Eliot's concept of the heroic and of the narrative task. Reconcilement may entail collapse, as at the end of *The Mill*; or the straining of the work towards unification may nevertheless result, as Edith Simcox wrote of *Daniel Deronda*, in a 'faithful transcript of the coexistence of unreconciled tendencies' (*Journal*, MS Bodley, p.60). Alongside George Eliot's respect for organicism, and her passionate need for interdependence, went an indefatigable awareness of misunderstanding and, equally, of the impossibility of writing within a single discourse. She suspected conclusions, which 'are at best negations'. She relished and distrusted metaphor, which displaces, disturbs hierarchy, and confuses fiction and material. We 'all get our thoughts entangled in metaphor'. So, in her response to other women writing, she distrusted emotion that all moved in one direction, easy sublimity, or argument which dissolved disagreeable incongruities.

Though some recent critics have set her work in opposition to Charlotte Brontë's, and Elaine Showalter even opposes her to George Sand, these are the two women writers she most admired in the 1850s. The new novel about which she writes with most fervent enthusiasm is Charlotte Brontë's *Villette*:

> I am only just returned to a sense of the real world about me for I have been reading Villette, a still more wonderful book than Jane Eyre. There is something almost preternatural in its power . . . . Yet what passion, what fire in her! Quite as much as in George Sand. (Haight, 1954, II, pp.87, 91)

43

George Eliot

The comparison is impressive, for to Marian Evans

> George Sand is the unapproached artist who, to Jean-
> Jacques' eloquence and deep sense of external nature, unites
> the clear delineation of character and the tragic depth of
> passion. (Pinney, 1963, p.55)

And Jean-Jacques Rousseau's confessions, she told
Emerson in 1848, 'had first awakened her to deep
reflection'. His work 'has sent that electric thrill through
my intellectual and moral frame which has awakened me
to new perceptions . . . —and this is not by teaching me
any new belief'. Ruby Redinger suggests that she had
discovered that 'what she most valued in creative
literature had little to do with intellectual power or even
literary artistry' but is rather 'a search for delineations
of human passion with which she could empathize'
(Redinger, 1976, p.153). But Redinger here composes
false contraries. George Eliot is seized by Rousseau's
doing away with 'duteous reticences; his power of
simultaneous utterance, analysis and enactment thrills
her (and we should remember that the 'electric thrill' had
a more precise and up-to-date significance for her than
for us). Intellectual power is manifested in the intense
fusion of utterance and experience.

To Redinger, 'when her genius was finally freed for
creative expression, it was to be restricted by her need to
analyse' (Redinger, 1976, p.151). Instead, I would assert
that the psychodrama of analysis in her work empowers
the passional: she gives access to the full intensity of
feeling by means of its analysis; an analysis which never
mistakenly obliterates or reconciles the multiple impulses within event, speech or knowledge. The 'psychological anatomy' of the early days of marriage in George
Sand's novel *Jacques* stirred George Eliot profoundly—

such study of the early days of marriage was to become one of her own deeply analysed expressions of 'everyday tragedy' in *Romola*, *Middlemarch* and *Daniel Deronda*.

This power of committed utterance (which may include concealment but is not inhibited by it) most excited her in George Sand, in Rousseau, and in Charlotte Brontë. She may the more have admired it because of the anonymity of her own production at the time and the wince of facetiousness with which she still balanced what disturbed her. Rousseau was to continue to play his part in her work, particularly in her reappraisal of the mentor figure. His views were in many ways antipathetic to her, particularly in his exclusion of 'la femme-auteur' and his distrust of education for women. But, as she had declared, it did not really matter to her if his views were 'miserably erroneous'; what she valued was his awakened language, which allowed him to tap unrecognised incentives, so that our impressions come not only from what he tells us but 'from what he unconsciously enables us to discern' (*Theophrastus Such*, I, p.7).

Her discussions of Geraldine Jewsbury's *Constance Herbert* and Bremer's *Hertha* (and her reading of Bremer's later novel, *Father and Daughter* (1859)) allow us to track the movement of desires and difficulties which will fuel George Eliot's own later work. We tend to overlook the creative importance of writers who are no longer much read; perhaps that is why the urgency of George Eliot's response to Jewsbury and Bremer has been ignored. Their novels concentrated George Eliot's attention on problems crucial in her own art.

One of the most enduring of these problems is *renunciation*, an act whose meaning changes, and which yet resists change, throughout her writing life. Another problem is the possibility of independent life for women, and the counter-claims of need and nurturing. She takes to task Geraldine Jewsbury for suggesting

> that what duty calls on us to renounce, will invariably prove 'not worth the keeping'; and if it *were* the fact, renunciation would cease to be moral heroism, and would be simply a calculation of prudence. (Pinney, 1963, p.134)

Her review (written, it is to be remembered, without indication that it is by a woman) pointed out that 'there is not a man in her book who is not either weak, perfidious, or rascally, while almost all of the women are models of magnanimity and devotedness' (ibid., p.135).

Balancing renunciation and resistance provides major dramatic encounters in George Eliot's novels: Romola leaving Tito and encountering Savonarola, Dorothea considering whether to carry on Casaubon's life-work. But she is not entirely fair to Geraldine Jewsbury in concentrating her comments on this one problem.

Quite as revealing is what George Eliot *excludes* from discussion (perhaps does not even notice or retain): Jewsbury's stringent and generous depiction of relationships between women. *Constance Herbert* lurches towards melodrama when men enter. But the subtle, even perception with which Jewsbury describes the long-growing relationship between Constance and her aunt, Margaret, and their friendship with Miss Wilmot, draws our attention to a singular absence in George Eliot's own writing: the study of female friendship.

Certainly in George Eliot's work, women from time to time save other women, as Dinah does Hetty, Aunt Glegg (in a limited way) Maggie, Dorothea Rosamond. But what we scarcely find recorded is the easy, loving equality which finds delight in each other's company for its own sake. Here Jewsbury excels. She excels also at those scrupulous observations poised on the edge of generalisation which we recognise as later one of George Eliot's most subtle narrative movements. There is a further powerful effect in Jewsbury's novel which sharply focuses for us what we shall *not* find in George Eliot's plots—what indeed would be an unthinkable conclusion to a George Eliot novel. Jewsbury's novel ends with Constance, single, independent, and satisfied to manage her own small estate. She has earlier, with great suffering, renounced marriage because of the hereditary madness of both sides of her family. Fredrika Bremer's novel *Father and Daughter* (whose title already suggests other parallels with George Eliot's work) ends in a similar vein. Rosa survives the loss of the man she loves to complete her father's life-work ('a bridge between the philosophy of paganism and Christianity') and to manage the family estate and farm on Gothland:

> her deep blue eye still retains its youthful brightness and serenity. Her life is a many-sided life of activity and love, both in spirit and in deed. (Bremer, 1859, p.339)

The conclusion of Bremer's book, despite the consolatory tone of the passage quoted, is both painful and impressive: painful because the degree of renunciation seems foolhardy, but impressive because we are presented with an image of a woman happy in her own resources and independent.

The epigraph to the book indicates its deepest knot, one which must have spoken particularly strongly to George Eliot at the beginning of her creative career after the death of her father: ' "Love compels, freedom binds more strongly than law" Rosa Norrby'. Or, as Rosa says later: 'My father gave me freedom, but he has bound my heart to him, and I cannot, and I will not break the bond' (Bremer, 1859, p.148). Bremer's novel, which opens in the study of the scholar-father who goes blind during the course of the novel and whose exigent love draws Rosa away from the hedonistic figure of her lover Axel, has clear connections with *Romola* and with *Middlemarch*—connections which are all the more telling for being fugitive and sometimes inverted in George Eliot's work. In *Romola* the hedonistic lover betrays: in *Middlemarch* he saves.

The figure of Bremer, an avowedly feminist writer, has considerable moral power in George Eliot's imagination, but she repudiates what she called Bremer's 'rank growth of sentimentality'. And in a revealing allusion continues, 'Nothing can be more curious than the combination in her novels of the vapourishly affected and unreal with the most solid Dutch sort of realism' (Pinney, 1963: p.331). In *Adam Bede* she sets out her own artistic goal as difficult truth-telling. 'Falsehood is so easy truth so difficult . . . . It is for this rare, precious quality of truth-telling that I delight in many Dutch paintings, which lofty-minded people despise' (I, p.268, ch.17).

George Eliot, in choosing to emphasise 'the hard drudgery of real practice' sought to distinguish her writing from one available feminist model, which, she felt, so overvalued aspiration as misleadingly to set aside difficulty and to betray those women who followed the path. Hertha 'for seven years . . . submits to the procrastination of her marriage, rather than rebel against her father in his last years' (Pinney, 1963: p.333) The speed of infatuation in *The Mill* is perhaps a riposte to this and other women's novels, with their insistence on control and delay. Marian Evans, who knew something of such sacrifice and such monstrous affection, distrusted any furbelows of sentiment which disguised the rocky path women set themselves when they chose to submit to parental demands rather than to rebel. So she doubted the pictures in Jewsbury and Bremer of the pleasures of renunciation and, perhaps for that reason, distrusted their images of independent life for women.

George Eliot intensely admired *Villette*, which concludes with an equivocal independence so aware of its own necessary losses that Charlotte Brontë allows the reader to choose whether M. Paul returned or not. That painful hesitancy, and obduracy, which requires the doubling of the ending in Charlotte Brontë, helps us to understand why George Eliot could never conclude with an image of independent life for a woman in her own fiction until the end of her career, although Romola becomes surrogate-mother-and-father to Tito's other family. Even Gwendolen's 'independence', such as it is, remains doubtful. Can she sustain it in magnanimity? Is the enlarged space she is to inhabit scorched or fruitful? We are not to know that story, and the not knowing, in itself, makes for doubt.

George Eliot saw that beneath the bland pastoralism of the independent woman on her estate with which Bremer and Jewsbury conclude their works, there lies disguised appalling loss, a loss which Charlotte Brontë recognised. This loss is sexual love. George Eliot's own plots suggest that she thought it too easy to proffer a life without anxiety or joy, achieved by giving up sexuality. Romola is as near as any of her women come to a satisfied renunciation of active sexual life, and she does it by adopting the role of Madonna, substituting quasi-motherly joys for fulfilling physical love. Towards the end of *Middlemarch* Dorothea finds herself, deeply distressed, in the position of the Bremer and Jewsbury heroines: financially independent, with altruistic projects, having renounced Will as unworthy. The last section of the book sweeps her on beyond that solution. The alternative solution has been emphatically incorporated in the book's argument, but it is not George Eliot's conclusion. It is engulfed and obliterated by sexual joy.

When we read George Eliot's narrative alongside the plots of other women writers at the time, we can see that the conclusion of Dorothea's marriage to Will (which has often disturbed readers) is not unconsidered, nor seeking easily to resolve difficulty. Rather, it is bringing openly to the test the difficulties left over or concealed in the 'too confident' conclusions of other women writers (Pinney, 1968, p.332). Before becoming a novelist herself, George Eliot commented on Miss Bremer's 'religious philosophy':

> When a novelist is quite sure that she has a theory which suffices to illustrate all the difficulties of our earthly existence, her novels are too likely to illustrate little else than her own theory. (Ibid.)

My argument should not be read as complete explanation or justification of George Eliot's endings. Far more factors will need to be taken into the discussion before any thorough appraisal of the fatalities of plot in her work can be reached. But it does serve to show that she lived artistically and emotionally within the debates created by women writers at the time.

Consider, for instance, her review of Holme Lee's *Kathie Brand*. (Holme Lee is a woman's pseudonym). This review sheds light on a number of the plot elements in *The Mill on the Floss* and makes it clear that she knew exactly what artistic risks she was taking in making Maggie a kind of ugly duckling who becomes a swan. (Dorothea, later, offers another reading of Andersen's tale: the ugly duckling becomes a swan but has to go on living among the ducks 'in the brown pond'.) She writes of *Kathie Brand* in 1857:

> The elements are precisely those we have had worked up into hundreds of stories—a plain child growing up, under adversity, into a fascinating woman, with whom everybody falls in love. (*Westminster Review*, 67, 1857, pp.320-1)

Then the creative irritation which feeds the story of Stephen and Maggie appears. Like Hertha, Kathie refuses to marry an ideal suitor 'after a seven years' courtship, because a fastidious and impossible dictate of duty suggests a refusal' (Ibid.) Maggie, in contrast, is swept away after brief acquaintance; her 'fastidious and impossible dictate of duty' involves a renunciation very different from that of Kathie who will be rewarded with her lover in the end his wife having meanwhile, 'opportunely', died. George Eliot concludes her review with a sentence that casts light forward on her artistic practice: 'When the imagination moves amidst ordinary realities, if it does not realize them vividly, the result is inevitable weariness'. The hidden resistances and enforcements of the works can be understood more subtly if we do not concentrate our attention within the 'great woman' model, but see the text as containing and resisting other writing by which it was surrounded. It allows us already to query Gilbert and Gubar's assertion that the narrator approves the 'struggle to attain the renunciation that alone can redeem human life from suffering' (Gilbert and Gubar, 1979, p.498). And a consciousness of intertextuality will prove particularly useable in reading *Middlemarch*, where the writing of others within the Victorian women's movement is confidently (and confidingly) alluded to within the narrative, creating a sub-text of debate.

## Chapter Three

# Putting on Man's Apparel: The Early Fiction

## *I*

The writing and the reading which George Eliot undertook before she began to write fiction gave her a repertoire, or grammar, of fictional relations which she could then refine into a particular style. *Scenes of Clerical Life*, because it is the most melodramatic and declarative of her works, has yielded striking insights to critics who have considered what the stories themselves indicate of desire and concealment. Diane Sadoff, Sandra Gilbert and David Carroll have all analysed the plots in this way.

Sadoff tracks in *Amos Barton* the configuration which most concerns her in George Eliot's fiction: 'father–daughter seduction . . . in which father and daughter are linked by the daughter's emerging desire and the story that narrates it' (Sadoff, 1982, p.66). Sadoff's initiating account of the events of *Amos Barton* acknowledges that 'Eliot's first story obscures its sexual meaning'. That meaning she figures as 'the daughter reaps the structural rewards of familial desire. The dying mother encourages her daughter to replace herself' (Ibid., p.67). Patty 'remains by her father's side, and makes the evening sunshine of his life'. The daughter, no longer substitute mother to her now-grown siblings, remains substitute wife and housekeeper to her father.

Survival in a work of fiction is no accident but is imbued with the writer's desire and will. Sadoff's reading of the text deliberately displaces Milly, the wife, from the centre of our attention. The resistance that George Eliot felt to Bremer's procrastination of marriage and devotion to the father may reinforce, rather than counter, Sadoff's insight. Marian Evans knew too well the lure of remaining 'substitute wife and house-keeper' and if, as Kristeva suggests, women write in order to re-work their family romance, we need not be surprised that this first story is weighted with a conclusion from which Evans herself had escaped. Very late in her life, after Lewes's death, she confided to Edith Simcox that the emotional track of her life had been that of the single, consuming relationship:

> she spoke half in self-reproach of the people who live in so many relations that their lives must always be full, whereas she always sent the strength of her feeling in one channel which absorbed it all. It had been so with her father. (*Journal*, Bodley MS. p.47. 29 April 1879).

We begin to understand perhaps why her counter-imaginative passion was for multiformity and multiplicity, the process she had quoted thankfully from MacKay: 'opening out the barren mystery of the one into more explicit and manageable forms'. It is this counter-process of invention and proliferation which Sadoff's chapter on George Eliot too little represents, though it analyses with considerable subtlety George Eliot's attempts to leave behind the father/daughter seduction.

The nature of Sadoff's Freudian method means that she is preoccupied with origins, an emotional and intellectual obsession which Freud shared with his immediate predecessors such as Darwin. The drive back towards origins, the Oedipus story, is increasingly satirised and evaded in George Eliot's late books— though it is not a drive which she can ever entirely lay to rest within herself, as the plots of her books, with their lost parents, keys to all mythologies, and cabbalistic learning, all demonstrate. What she does do is *recognise* the drive, both in herself and in her culture, and counter it with an equally intense movement towards differentiation, expansion, lateral kinning, fostering and foster-parenting, and sympathetic generalisation, which all create new and multiple relationships. In *Scenes of Clerical Life*, as their brief scope itself indicates, such a movement has only just begun; the imagination's plumbing towards an origin identified with the father still prevails. Karen Greenberg has emphasised the critical obsession with the Oedipus myth and has linked that myth to the reinforcement of patriarchy. The myth which meant most to George Eliot was that of Antigone, resisting the authority of the king–uncle. Gilbert and Guber suggest that:

> these *Scenes* only partly deal with three representative mild-mannered clergymen, since their drama actually depends upon quite extraordinary women. The stories told by Eliot are ignored by most critics in favor of the morals she expounds, in part because these plots are almost embarr-assingly melodramatic. But such plots reveal a striking pattern of authorial vengeance in the service of female

submission that informs Eliot's later fiction. (Gilbert and Gubar, 1979, p.484)

Their suggestion that the women are 'extraordinary' is double-edged. As long as the narrator is cast as masculine and of a higher social class, 'extraordinariness' has an element of the concessive. Rather, George Eliot portrays the power and scale of ordinary experience, ordinary women. The women characters are contrasted with class-ridden women readers who fail to read them truly:

> 'An utterly uninteresting character!' I think I hear a lady reader exclaim—Mrs Farthingale, for example, who prefers the ideal in fiction; to whom tragedy means ermine tippets, adultery, and murder; and comedy, the adventures of some personage who is quite a 'character'. (Amos Barton, I, p.66, ch.5)

## II

'George Eliot' did not remain male for long. Very soon that name meant a known female source of writing, just as it did with George Sand. There was no need to change the name: the name changed its signification. While the pretence of maleness was under threat she wrote (Haight, 1978, VIII, pp.238-9) to Annie Leigh Smith, Barbara Leigh Smith Bodichon's sister, to thank her for having said, 'I am more glad of Adam Bede because it is yours.' The letter is one of her earliest and most revealing allusions to her difficulties as a woman writing. She has recourse to the exotic, playful discourse of *The Arabian Nights* to formulate her dilemma.

> Yesterday I had reason to foresee the great need I should have of the Princess Parizade's cotton wool in my ears, lest

certain noises should distract me from going steadily along
my way. (Ibid.)

These 'noises' represent the controversy surrounding
the reception of *Adam Bede* and the discussion of its
authorship.

It is worth dwelling on the story to which George Eliot
refers because it so clearly forms an 'unconscious
allegory' of her own history and position. Princess
Parizade is the heroine of 'The Two Sisters', a story
placed last in some versions of *The Arabian Nights*. The
tale has elements which gain a particular warmth later in
George Eliot's career; for example, the figure of the good
foster-father, here of Princess Parizade and her brothers:
'he attached himself to them entirely; he watched over
their rising years with the solicitude of a real parent.'

The story is one of inordinate, fantastic and playful
desires—desires which are eventually not disappointed
but fulfilled. An old woman comes to Princess Parizade
when she reaches puberty, and puts wishes in her mind:
wishes for the talking bird, the golden water, and the
singing tree.

> The first is the talking bird, who, not only can talk and
> reason like us, but as a bird can call all the singing birds in his
> neighbourhood to come and join his song. The second is the
> singing tree, the leaves of which are so many mouths, which
> form a most harmonious concert. The third is the golden
> water, a small quantity of which being put into a basin, fills
> it, and forms a beautiful fountain, which continually plays
> without ever overflowing.' (*Arabian Nights*, 1792, IV, p.221)

Bird, tree and fountain offer reason, knowledge, voice,
community, variety, plenitude, and female and male
fertility in the images of the basin and the fountain.
Parizade's two brothers set out to gain the objects, but

the first fails through fear, the second through combativeness, both deflected by

> innumerable voices, bursting out as it seemed from under the earth. Of these, some ridiculed, some abused, and others threatened him . . . in voices calculated to inspire shame, anger, and dismay. (Ibid., p.226)

The brothers are turned to stone. So Parizade sets out. 'She lost no time in fruitless grief; *but putting on man's apparel*, she mounted a horse and took the same road her brothers had done' (ibid., pp.229–30; emphasis added). She stuffed her ears with cotton so that 'all she perceived was one confused noise' (p.231). As she came in sight of the bird, one of the plugs fell out of her ear.

> The threatenings and execrations, which she now heard distinctly, were terrible. The bird himself, in a voice more tremendous than all of them, called out for her to go back. (p.231)

But she goes on. She seizes the bird of knowledge, who then aids her, and she takes the little plant and the 'little silver flagon' which, once returned to her house, become immediately a great tree and a fountain 20 feet high.

The courage of the daughter, beset by threatening voices, refusing to turn back, using guile, masculine disguise and common sense, to seize knowledge, beauty and fulfilment, ravishes the reader. 'It is a beautiful story', writes George Eliot. In life, such unchequered completeness cannot be attained except *through* story. George Eliot's stories later attempt both to offer plenitude and to keep faith with difficulty.

We need not allegorise her reception of this tale too stably, but we can understand more fully by its means the richness of symbolic need to which it answered. Like

Antigone, like Parizade, obduracy is a talisman for her against disappointment and self-betrayal. Once the tale is read and half-recalled, it allows the fugitive satisfactions of narrative to be supplemented by those long-held images which are most remembered because most desired. The story is at the extreme end of a spectrum of feeling about the need for deafness and the need for hearing which continues throughout her work. Parizade deafens herself in order finally to hear the bird, the tree and the fountain. Her deafness keeps her intact, uninvaded by hostile voices. The joyous harmony reached is akin to Maggie Tulliver's metaphor for her own life; she had wanted always 'more instruments playing together'. At the far end of that same spectrum is the famous passage from *Middlemarch* which may well echo again this particular story, of Parizade 'wadding' her ears in order to survive. In *Middlemarch* it is tempered by being combined with elements drawn from quite other sources, such as Huxley's essay on 'The Physical Basis of Life':

> If we had a keen vision and feeling of all ordinary life, it would be like hearing the grass grow and the squirrel's heart beat, and we should die of that roar which lies on the other side of silence. As it is, the quickest of us walk about well wadded with stupidity. (*Middlemarch*, I, ch.20)

## II

In *Adam Bede*, Hetty is likened to Memnon's statue which plays music only when touched by particular rays of the sun. In this discussion of female figures and male voices, it is with *Adam Bede* that I conclude. After the publication of that novel George Eliot's identity became known, and she bid farewell to her male persona by means of the depressive first-person male narrator of *The Lifted Veil* who foresees his own death and experiences it within the story. *Adam Bede* is, then, the one fully achieved novel in which the masculine narrator is still an intact fiction, a sealed (though intermittent) level of the discourse. This dramatised male narrator can confidently set himself apart from the characters. He appears, to master as well as to sympathise with them. In this work George Eliot set out to revise a powerful female text, that of Elizabeth Gaskell's *Ruth*. Her enterprise had delicately to distinguish itself from common assumptions, as well as to question *Ruth's* idealisation. This is not to say that her design was pondered and combative but that she tried again, as with Fredrika Bremer, to find a means of *realising*, not aggrandising, the face of ordinary tragedy.

*Adam Bede*, on its first publication, roused immense interest, both as a work whose reflectiveness eschewed the usual idealisations of pastoral, and as a work without a known provenance. The question of who was 'George Eliot' was debated as if it must change or control the meaning of the book. Was it by a clergyman?—'He is evidently a country clergyman' (*Saturday Review*, Carroll, 1971, p.73). By a man or a woman? Jane Welsh Carlyle jokingly imagined the author lighting his pipe with her letter of appreciation. A vigorous correspondence was conducted on the matter in *The Times*. Dickens 'waved all men away from *Adam Bede*, and nailed my colours to the Mast with "Eve" upon them' (ibid., p.85). He praised particularly the conception of Hetty's character as 'skilful, determined, and uncompromising'. E.S. Dallas ends his magisterial review of the book in *The Times*: 'Nobody seems to know who is Mr George Eliot, and when his previous work appeared it was even surmised that he must be a lady' (Ibid., 84). Anne Mozley is quite sure it is 'from a female pen':

> The time is past for any felicity, force, or freedom of expression to divert our suspicions on this head; if women will write under certain conditions, perhaps more imperatively required from them than from men, as well as more difficult of attainment, it is proved that a wide range of human nature lies open to their comprehension. (Ibid., p.90)

This distant controversy may now seem remote, since, with the confidence of retrospect, we take for granted that *Adam Bede* is 'from a female pen'. But the sequestration of an origin for the work has its effects in the book's composition. The comparison with framed pictures acquires a special meaning. The frame completes, compacts and excludes. George Eliot was bent on finding a proper scale for writing, a scale which, like Ruskin and the pre-Raphaelites, would pay so intense a respect to detail that detail could figure both as contingency and as parable. The writing should *work*, through description, through analysis, through rumination. It should be a part of the working world it describes. It should guarantee its own authenticity by making the reader aware of it as labour and as pleasure. Anne Mozley remarks that 'the position of the writer towards every point in discussion is a woman's position, that is, from a stand of observation rather than more active participation' (ibid.). Shrewd as this comment is as a description of the place assigned to women comfortably by the society she inhabited, it does not sufficiently register the extent to which the writing declares itself as participation in the society described, and participation in labour.

The participation is expressed in class terms, and with an allusion to pre-Raphaelite precision. A description near the book's beginning turns away from any raising, or blurring, into a discourse which draws on the 'realism' of Ruskin. ('Realism' was itself at this time a newly-coined word.)

> Doubtless there was a large sweep of park and a broad glassy pool in front of that mansion, but the swelling slope of meadow would not let our traveller see them from the village green. He saw instead a foreground which was just as lovely—the level sunlight lying like transparent gold among the gently-curving stems of the feathered grass and the tall red sorrel, and the white umbels of the hemlocks lining the busy hedgerows. It was that moment in summer when the sound of the scythe being whetted makes us cast more lingering looks at the flower-sprinkled tresses of the meadows. (I, p.23, ch.2)

The passage is composed of details, some of them intensified by tranquil recollections of Keats: 'Not so much life as on a summer's day/ Robs not one light seed from the feathered grass': and 'hemlocks', whose 'white umbels' are here given their botanical description. The 'swelling slope of meadow' shuts out a view of the upper-class parkland: in that word, 'swelling', and at the other end of the passage, 'tresses', there is a faint suggestion of a female body. Poised between the two words is the 'tall red sorrel'. It is to be some pages yet before we reach the first reference to that 'poor wandering lamb Hetty Sorrel' as Dinah calls her. The closeness of her surname to sorrow has been often remarked, but we are first presented with the word as plant-name. The reader is drawn into the passage, first as a traveller, and then, in a more generous sharing of experience, in first-person plural. We are joined in a knowledge which is both ominous and yet reassuringly repetitive: 'the sound of the scythe being whetted' is there to 'presage the grasses fall', but also, in this work, Hetty's fall. One could emphasise the Biblical and Marvellian traces in that last sentence; they function without needing to be more than summoned to the surface. The description ends with the sense of approaching change and of shorn meadows. The passage is serenely precise and it is only in retrospect that we become aware that it is less contingent, more parabolic, than at first appears. It works first as picture, framed and composed. But it works also as narrative, restless with unseen consequence.

In the chosen scale of this work, meaning can emerge best from 'the drudgery of real practice', though in this passage pleasure is more evident than drudgery. Old Lisbeth Bede first perceives Dinah as an angel, but then with earnest relief, she sees 'the traces of labour from her childhood upwards' in her hands, and exclaims: '"Why, you're a working woman!" "Yes, I am Dinah Morris, and I work in the cotton-mill when I am at home" ' (I, p.161, ch.10).

Dinah Morris, Methodist preacher, mill-worker, doubly a working woman, fully occupied both in Stonyshire and Loamshire, was the figure from whom George Eliot derived much of the energy of the book. In writing it, she referred to it as 'my aunt's story'. The biographical incentive becomes part of the book's theme, which is George Eliot's first major exploration of kinship, the tangle of unchosen relationships which entrap and sustain the individual:

> Family likeness has often a deep sadness in it. Nature, that great tragic dramatist, knits us together by bone and muscle, and divides us by the subtler web of our brains; blends yearning and repulsion; and ties us by our heart-string to the beings that jar us at every movement. We hear

a voice with the very cadence of our own uttering the thoughts we despise; we see eyes—ah! so like our mother's—averted from us in cold alienation; and our last darling child startles us with the air and gestures of the sister we parted from in bitterness long years ago. The father to whom we owe our best heritage—the mechanical instinct, the keen sensibility to harmony, the unconscious skill of the modelling hand—galls us, and puts us to shame by his daily errors; the long-lost mother, whose face we begin to see in the glass as our own wrinkles come, once fretted our young souls with her anxious humours and irrational persistence. (I, p.55–56, ch.4)

The knitting of willed and unwilled in family ties, and in procreation, enmeshes the characters in the action.

The extended 'kinship' of the quasi-feudal community is shown to be in great measure factitious. 'No gentleman, out of a ballad, could marry a farmer's niece,' thinks Arthur to himself. Paternalism is threatened by the blood-kinning across class between Arthur Donnithorne and Hetty. The familial metaphor in class-structure can survive only if it abides by its patriarchal, vertical model of kinship, with the squire as father and the villagers as children. The oppressiveness of this 'naturalised' organisation is shown when the alternative *lateral* model of kinship is used: brothers and sisters, love-matches, cousinage. Dinah is the principle of that alternative kinship,

She makes connections, traverses distances. She is the only person in the book who can travel freely, and without disastrous consequences. This mobility is opposed to the heavy weighting of other characters in the book to remain 'in their place', a place so articulated that they can each speak only in terms of their own labour. Adam speaks in carpentry images, Mrs Poyser in images of the dairy, while Hetty—never herself articulate and given remarkably little direct speech until her scene of absolute declaration in prison—is described in terms of young animals:

> the beauty of young frisking things, round-limbed, gambolling, circumventing you with a false air of innocence—the innocence of a young star-browed calf, for example. (pp. 122-3, ch. 7)

The tension in the book's own procedure is between framing, perfecting and completing (the pastoral impulse), and narrative movement with its dangers and freedom, its possibilities for radical change. The wonderful 'scenes' that all readers recollect—'The Workshop', 'The Games', 'The Harvest Supper', for example—celebrate completeness. The book opens with Adam's demand that the men work past the clock:

> 'I can't abide to see men throw away their tools i' that way, the minute the clock begins to strike, as if they took no pleasure i' their work, and was afraid o' doing a stroke too much.' (I, p. 6, ch. 1)

Adam's unbendingness, his woodenness, his zeal for completion and perfecting, are openly admired in this scene, and then brought into the stress of narrative event as the book proceeds. The pastoral of this book is a pastoral of work, and one in which the novelist shares. Kathleen Blake in her discussion of 'Middlemarch and the Woman Question' (Blake, 1976, pp. 285-312) points out the extent to which the narrative discourse in that book dwells on the problem of 'indefiniteness' or 'indeterminacy' for women. What tasks are to be done? 'Not to shape the world is to be shapeless oneself, which for natures conscious of shaping energy means painful consciousness of their own dispersal' (ibid., pp. 293-4). The pleasurability of the text in *Adam Bede* derives from its fullness of project, its having found a shape for activity. Yet within it also is a process of discovering that any delimited project is in danger of self-enclosure, that the framed picture, the pastoral, and the enclosed family must leave out or exclude too much. So, description must become the medium of doubt. Plenty, in this discourse, is to be set at the service of ordinary life: 'human feeling . . . does not wait for beauty—it flows with resistless force and brings beauty with it' (I, p.269, ch.17).

> Paint us an angel, if you can, with a floating violet robe, and a face paled by the celestial light; paint us yet oftener a Madonna, turning her mild face upward and opening her arms to welcome the divine glory; but do not impose on us any aesthetic rules which shall banish from the region of Art those old women scraping carrots with their work-torn hands, those heavy clowns taking holiday in a dingy pothouse, those rounded backs and stupid weather-beaten faces that have bent over the spade and done the rough work of the world—those homes with their tin pans, their brown pitchers, their rough curs, and their clusters of onions. (I, p.270, ch.17)

'The old woman bending over her flower-pots, or eating her solitary dinner' is not, in fact, prominent in *Adam Bede* though she is there perhaps in the figure of Lisbeth. Instead, the emphasis is upon the younger and comelier members of the community, and 'the rare, precious quality of truthfulness' is sought through disentangling false models from actual behaviour. One of the most high-spirited sources of pleasure in the work is the recording of 'country-talk' like that of the unidealising Bartle Massey with his diatribe against women and their ineffectiveness.

## George Eliot

'It's the silliest lie a sensible man like you ever believed, to
say a woman makes a house comfortable. It's a story got up,
because women are there, and something must be found for
'em to do. I tell you there isn't a thing under the sun that
needs to be done at all, but what a man can do better than a
woman, unless it's bearing children, and they do that in a
poor make-shift way; it had better ha' been left to the men.'
(I, p.361, ch.21)

Truthfulness is the procedure of describing, and
simultaneously of troubling, description. Hetty's disori-
ented journey acts out in narrative such troubling of the
foreknown. The language of the novelist attempts to

give a faithful account of men and things as they have
mirrored themselves in my mind. The mirror is doubtless
defective; the outlines will sometimes be disturbed, the
reflection faint and confused; but I feel as much bound to tell
you as precisely as I can *what that reflection is, as if I were in the
witness-box narrating my experience on oath.* (emphasis added) (I,
pp.265–66, ch.17)

The mirror in the narrator's mind re-uses the description of Hetty's mirror, the one she rejects because of the
'numerous dim blotches sprinkled over the mirror' in her
room: being fixed in an upright position it gives only 'one
good view of her head and neck' (I, p.223, ch.15). Her
secret glass '(a small red-framed shilling looking glass,
without blotches' (I, p.223)) Hetty considers to give a
more truthful likeness. The two mirrors, one blotched,
one diminished, are set against (and yet suggest the
difficulty of ever believing) the mirror in the mind.
Hetty recognises only a diminished image of herself,
framed (perhaps over-significantly) in red, and corre-
sponding to Arthur Donnithorne's fantasising of her as
'a veritable Hebe'. The mirror's frame excludes her body.

She remains ignorant of her full physical self; though responsive to its needs, she is utterly unreflective. The narrator's metaphors suggest allusions to Hetty and her story, in part backward-looking, in part proleptic. The kinning of discourse and character is crucial to an understanding of Hetty's significance in the book. If Dinah is the source of biographic energy, Hetty is the source of imaginative energy—and the energies are twinned.

Hetty's unreflectiveness is set in contrast to Dinah's unselfconsciousness. Dinah, preaching, is unembarrassed by any sense that she is 'a lovely young woman on whom men's eyes are fixed' (I, p.136, ch.8). In her bedroom, next to Hetty's, there is immediately a window instead of a double mirror:

> the first thing she did on entering the room, was to seat herself in this chair, and look out on the peaceful fields beyond which the large moon was rising, just above the hedgerow elms. (I, p.234, ch.15)

Her gaze is outward. No commentary points out to us that she, also, is looking on her double: the moon. Diana is peaceably regarded by Dinah who is held safe outside classical learning within her own religious knowledge. She is also, of course, brooding on Hetty, her double. The moon, here large and steady, is also linked to women's periodicity and Diana is the goddess of childbirth. (The whole of this chapter has striking similarities to George Eliot's very first piece of fiction published in 1847 in the *Coventry Herald and Observer* as part of her series 'Poetry and Prose, From the Notebook of an Eccentric' which opens: 'In very early times indeed, when no maidens had looking glasses, except the mermaidens, there lived in a deep valley two hamadryads.' One is narcissistic, one cares for the living things she sees in the pond.)

The word 'reflection' has multiple meaning in *Adam Bede*: the woman looks into her mirror; the quasi-male narrator has a mirror in his mind. She is trapped by her reflection. The reflection is 'faint or confused': reflective thought, memory revived, image and water stir within the term. Hetty at the end of her wanderings seeks only a pool in which to drown herself, and in all the description of its 'wintry depth' she never looks into it. She feels, as she wakes, a moment of 'passionate joy in life . . . escaping from the brink of the cold black death in the pool'. The narrator in this earlier passage feels 'bound to tell you as precisely as I can what that reflection is, as if I were in the witness-box narrating my experience on oath' (I, p.265-6, ch.17).

One of the most compelling later sections of the narrative is the series of stories told by witnesses on oath, by means of which we piece together what happened to Hetty and her baby. The story is given its poignant full telling in the scene between Dinah and Hetty in prison when Hetty at last can recognise her own experience. Hetty reveals that she had reached a place where there was no water (II, p.250, ch.45) and had almost covered up the baby with chippings and then gone back for it the next day because she couldn't leave it: ' "I turned back the way I'd come. I couldn't help it, Dinah; it was the baby's crying made me go: and yet I was frightened to death" ' (II, p.251). Her confession ends with the cry: ' "Dinah, do you think God will take away that crying and the place in the wood, now I've told everything?" ' (p.252). The pleasure of pastoral framing has turned into the nightmare fixed images of remorse. Hetty, like the narrator, is left 'dreading nothing except falsity', urged on by the need to tell all truth.

The broken, interrupted and agonised narrative of Hetty's experience proves to be the major story that the book must tell, and only Dinah among the characters is permitted to hear it fully. The visual image of the mirror which (as in Gwendolen's later experience) is entrapping, is replaced by the accord of voice, a woman telling and a woman listening, traversing the bounds of locked reflection.

In earlier scenes, the effect of natural limits is retained and the emphasis on fulfilling occupations—living completely in the space available to you—reinforces an organicist view of society (Shuttleworth, 1984). But the two young women, Hetty and Dinah, break these limits and range across them, one supported by values which provide her with pathways, one unknowingly and vagrantly. Yet that vagrancy is as crucial as is the clear path to the imaginative project of the work. At the beginning of the book, there is a very strong contractual element: master and man, mother and son, writer and reader. Each knows his place and must fulfil it. But the narrative pries apart these fixed relations, allying itself with movement and suffering and change, even while it celebrates and records recurrence, endurance and restoration.

Many critics have found fault with George Eliot's presentation of Hetty, seeing it as ungenerous and rebuffing in its insistence on her small scope, her paucity of love, her vanity. But the treatment of Hetty is also a radical challenge to stereotypical portrayals of virgins and fallen women. Hetty demanded of George Eliot a considerable imaginative reach, which she expressed, as so often, in musical imagery. The narrative recognises the sexual aggression which not only men but women also harbour in their attraction to beings like Hetty (I, p. 121, ch. 7). Hetty is voluptuous physical life, her flesh and the butter she makes seeming at times lexically interchangeable:

> And they are the prettiest attitudes and movements into which a pretty girl is thrown in making up butter—tossing movements that give a charming curve to the arm, and a sideward inclination of the round white neck; little patting and rolling movements with the palm of the hand, and nice adaptations and finishings which cannot at all be effected without a great play of the pouting mouth and the dark eyes. And then the butter itself seems to communicate a fresh charm—it is so pure, so sweet-scented; it is turned off the mould with such a beautiful firm surface, like marble in a pale yellow light! Moreover, Hetty was particularly clever at making up the butter. (I, p.123, ch.7)

The passage equivocates about the extent of Hetty's self-consciousness, but certainly never ascribes to her the kind of absolute unknowing innocence that is attributed to the heroine in Elizabeth Stone's *The Young Seamstress* or in Elizabeth Gaskell's *Ruth*. Hetty's passion is physical and self-directed, not sustained by moral endurance. Her plight is, therefore, George Eliot suggests, *worse* than that of the high-minded heroines with inner resources who were the Victorian liberal version of fallen women (Mitchell, 1981, pp.6–69).

Marian Evans read Mrs Gaskell's *Ruth* in the same month that she read *Villette* (February 1853) and commented on it in a letter that concludes with chilling remarks on the position and prospects of women, who, she suggests, though legally disadvantaged, do not yet deserve much better. Her position on the law relating to women was to change entirely under the influence of Bessie Rayner Parkes and Barbara Bodichon, and was indeed to provide the narrative knot for each of her books after *Romola*; but her view of *Ruth*, its limitations and achievements, does not seem to have changed. The criticism of *Ruth's* sharp contrasts and of its idealisation served as a model which could be implicitly corrected in *Adam Bede*.

Hetty is *not* endowed with a rich inner life. Quite the contrary. She has little loving impulse, and receives little love from others. Her position in the Poyser household is ill-defined and her relationship to her charge, the dreadful Totty, cool on both sides:

> Hetty went close to the rocking-chair, and stood without her usual smile, and without any attempt to entice Totty, simply waiting for her aunt to give the child into her hands.
>
> 'Wilt go to cousin Hetty, my dilling, while mother gets ready to go to bed? Then Totty shall go into mother's bed, and sleep there all night.'
>
> Before her mother had done speaking, Totty had given her answer in an unmistakable manner, by knitting her brow, setting her tiny teeth against her under-lip, and leaning forward to slap Hetty on the arm with her utmost force. Then, without speaking, she nestled to her mother again. (I, p.219, ch.14)

The narrative commentary, with its insistent 'poor child' for Hetty, makes it clear that she and Tottie are kin in more sense than one. But Hetty is in the world of work, and finds an 'indefiniteness' in her place (unlike the other characters). Her only skill is making butter. Her hedonistic presence, so much at odds with George Eliot's ideals, is yet the most stirring imaginatively to the novelist. Technically, Hetty's experience focuses the problem of scale. George Eliot must avoid either pastoralising or enlarging her.

She is also the character whose depiction makes the greatest difficulty for the gender of the narrative discourse. The maleness of the narrator is dramatised in relation to Hetty in ways that are sometimes awkward or absurd, but which point to the difficulties of distinguishing between imagining and physically creating—difficulties particularly acute for the woman writer, writing purportedly as a man. Who made Hetty pregnant?

> Poor wandering Hetty, with the rounded childish face, and the hard unloving despairing soul looking out of it—with the narrow heart and narrow thoughts, no room in them for any sorrows but her own, and tasting that sorrow with the more intense bitterness! My heart bleeds for her as I see her toiling along on her weary feet, or seated in a cart, with her eyes fixed vacantly on the road before her, never thinking or caring whither it tends, till hunger comes and makes her desire that a village may be near . . . .
>
> God preserve you and me from being the beginners of such misery! (II, p.153, ch.37)

Hetty is abandoned by the male characters, including Adam:

> 'then, that's the deepest curse of all . . . that's what makes the blackness of it . . . *it can never be undone!* My poor Hetty . . . she can never be my sweet Hetty again . . . the prettiest thing God had made—smiling up at me . . . I thought she loved me . . . and was good'. (II, pp.203-4, ch.41)

Finally the male narrator sacrifices her, allowing her to die, accompanied always by the demonstrative tag 'poor Hetty'. The narrator sacrifices also Dinah, forbidden, with other women, to preach by a decision of the Wesleyan conference. Only Seth stands out against the rightness of this judgement. The narrative here can claim its signification from history: this is what happened at the Wesleyan conference. But it feeds too gratefully into the stabilising and making private with which the book regains its poise. Dinah no longer travels. She is contained within the family, back in the conventional ordering. So at the end of the book we are left with genre-painting and the frame restored; Dinah and Adam, with their daughter and their son, Uncle Seth and Colonel Donnithorne restored to his inheritance and exonerated of any knowledge of Hetty's death. The narrator withdraws, leaving the characters to compose the close.

Did George Eliot feel uneasy with her conclusion? Is that why she said that conclusions are at best negations? Certainly, the ending of *Adam Bede* diminishes energies and seals the picture with a layer of varnish. It satisfies, but it satisfies as acquiescence. During the course of the book the twin figures of Dinah and of Hetty have disturbed George Eliot creatively; Hetty, as I have shown, permeates the language of narration, refusing to be inscribed and contained, teasing the author's project. That irritation and difficulty drew George Eliot back again and again to related figures—Bertha, Rosamond, and finally Gwendolen, in whom selfishness becomes a principle of self-discovery and intelligence.

Elizabeth Gaskell had endowed her heroine with her own honeymoon journey; the charming and righteous stamina of Ruth at first begs questions about her awareness of her own sexual arousal, making her seem too blanched a figure to bear the weight of subsequent story, and then the work demands of her at the end a quite distasteful death, nursing her former lover. Yet in the high spirits and in the unselfconscious closeness of Gaskell to the story she told, George Eliot was faced with a challenge, as well as a chance to revise. George Eliot's assumed maleness means that *Adam Bede* has none of that outspoken sisterhood between writer and character which cost the woman Elizabeth Gaskell dear and which forced Victorian readers into reappraisal.

## III

Displacement was always important to George Eliot's creativity, whether as pseudonym, as metaphor, or as images of foster-parenting. But after this period she turned away with relief from the strain of suppression and deceit involved in concealing the (social) relationship of writer and writing. When she contrasts Hetty with her inward gaze and Dinah with her outward, there is in the narrative a dramatisation of an authorial problem:

> It made a strange contrast to see that sparkling self-engrossed loveliness looked at by Dinah's calm pitying face, with its open glance which told that her heart lived in no cherished secrets of its own, but in feelings which it longed to share with all the world. (I, p.210, ch.14)

That contrast of inward self-collusive gaze and outward, sisterly gaze registers a participation in both which teases and troubles the writer.

In these first works, *Scenes* and *Adam Bede*, George Eliot is developing the central theme of her work: that commonplace life is heroic, requires no raising to be remarkable, but does require a special quality of attention if its significance is to be truly observed. An important influence here is her experience in translating and thus taking part in the thought of Feuerbach with his insistence on human qualities as the measure for all experience, and on imagination as the 'limitless activity of the senses' (*The Essence of Christianity*, 1854). Feuerbach argues that humankind impoverishes itself by falsely setting overagainst humanity and ascribing to God precisely those human qualities we most value. Theology, he says, mistakes quantitative difference for qualitative difference:

> The divine being is nothing else than the human being, or, rather the human nature . . . made objective—i.e. contemplated and revered as another, a distinct being. (Feuerbach, 1854, p.14)

Recognition of human meaning is achieved by self-consciousness, by becoming aware of the self as typical, as well as individual. The imagination's power is the 'negativing of limits' 'which furnishes free space for the play of my feelings'.

This quality of *recognition*—not change of quality, but doing away with the limits of self—Feuerbach sees as the one true religious activity:

> We succeed only in what we do willingly; joyful effort conquers all things. But that is joyful activity which is in accordance with our nature, which we do not feel as a limitation, and consequently not as a constraint. And the happiest, the most blissful activity is that which is productive. To read is delightful, reading is passive activity; but to produce what is worthy to be read is more delightful still. (Ibid., 215-16)

These are George Eliot's words as well as Feuerbach's. She was moved by his views, turning to them for reassurance, particularly at the time she went to live with Lewes. She resisted Strauss's de-mythologising even while she translated his *Life of Jesus*, but she found in Feuerbach's emphasis on awakened imagination rather than change of scale an idea that helped to liberate her own creativity. In the joint enterprise of production she 'furnishes space' for the activity of reader and writer together.

By studying George Eliot's activity in translating Feuerbach, we apprehend the particular meaning that 'sympathy' had for her. In her essay 'The Natural History of German Life' (1856) she writes:

> A picture of human life such as a great artist can give, surprises even the trivial and the selfish into that attention to what is apart from themselves, which may be called the raw material of moral sentiment. When Scott takes us into Luckie Mucklebackit's cottage, or tells the story of 'The Two Drovers',—when Wordsworth sings to us the reverie of 'Poor Susan',—when Kingsley shows us Alton Locke gazing yearningly over the gate which leads from the highway into the first wood he ever saw,—when Hornung paints a group of chimney-sweepers,—more is done towards linking the higher classes with the lower, towards obliterating the vulgarity of exclusiveness, than by hundreds of sermons and philosophical dissertations. (Pinney, 1968, pp.270-1)

This is the activity of 'negativing limits' without any suggestion of transgression. So the study of framing and fulfilling, and of journeying and traversing, in *Adam Bede* is a study of two differing imaginative modes. Both correspond to George Eliot's artistic needs as a woman writing fiction secretly, across categories. The reader is first introduced in to the text as independent traveller, remains as observer, and then must travel alongside. The novel studies community, which is concerned with bounds as well as with connection. The narrative voice expresses the effort of reach, and tries both to accept and to outgo his separation. The characters are recognised, in an attempt at the kind of objectivity which will revere another as 'a distinct being'. But that 'distinctness' creates problems in the text; the sense of traversing, in

which reader and writer engage, makes us strongly
aware of class and cultural gaps in the work. Narrative
metaphor is here a passageway from the cultural
experience shared by author and readers to the
narrower range of the characters. So when Mrs Poyser
ceases scolding Dinah on hearing of Thias's drowning
the commentary swoops in too gratifyingly:

> 'Perhaps I can be of use to her, so I have fetched my bonnet
> and am going to set out.'
> 'Dear heart, dear heart! But you must have a cup o' tea first,
> child,' said Mrs Poyser, falling at once from the key of B with
> five sharps to the frank and genial C. (I, p.138, ch.8)

There is no to-and-fro movement. The characters
cannot move into the commentary's privileged space,
which we are invited to share. George Eliot's enterprise
is to escape from 'the influence of traditions and
prepossessions', but at this stage the narrative still
sometimes needles the reader apologetically, in
Thackerayan style:

> Considering these things, we can hardly think Dinah and
> Seth beneath our sympathy, accustomed as we may be to
> weep over the loftier sorrows of heroines in satin boots and
> crinoline, and of heroes riding fiery horses, themselves
> ridden by still more fiery passions. (I, p.53, ch.3)

The uneasiness of separation and of joining is intensified
by the necessary doubling of voice in the ostentatiously
male narrator. The deliberate adoption of 'man's apparel'
at this stage in her career made George Eliot particularly
aware of women's voices and women's bodies, and of her
own concealed relation to them. She is dramatising the
'man's sentence' from time to time in her writing,
particularly at moments of quasi-spoken voice, in which

the reader is addressed as you. The model of masculinity that she adopts at such moments is that of Thackeray, whose own elliptical ironies can harbour further equivocations of voice. Yet more often she is writing without any specified gender, as writing without provenance. She is coming to the end of the period of masculine disguise, but it was a period which had forced her to think about whether there were general distinctions between male and female voice.

In her next published work, the teller of his own tale is a man. The tale proved to be her vengeance on the male narrator and perhaps on her own subterfuge. Three times in the course of her writing career George Eliot used first-person narrative. All three cases are minor works, but they span her career. In each case the first-person narrator is male. The works are 'From the Notebook of an Eccentric' (1846), 'The Lifted Veil' (1859), and *The Impressions of Theophrastus Such* (1879).

Of these the first and last are collected essays, connected by the narrator. 'The Lifted Veil' she described as 'not a *jeu d'esprit,* but a *jeu de melancolie'.* In each case, the narrator is valetudinarian, weakened by insight. In 'The Notebook of an Eccentric' these qualities are doubled in the dead friend, Macarthy, whom the writer alone mourns:

> He seemed to have a preternaturally sharpened vision, which saw knots and blemishes, where all was smoothness to others. The unsightly condition of the masses—their dreary ignorance—the conventional distortion of human nature in the upper classes—the absence of artistic harmony and beauty in the details of outward existence, were with him not merely themes for cold philosophy, indignant philippics, or pointed satire; but positively painful elements in his experience, sharp iron entering his soul. Had his nature been less noble, his benevolence less God-like, he

would have been a misanthropist, all compact of bitter sarcasm, and therefore no poet. As it was, he was a humourist,—one who sported with all forms of human life, as if they were so many May-day mummings, uncouth, monstrous disguises of poor human nature, which has not discovered its dignity. (Pinney, 1963, p.15)

This is the nightmare face of sympathy.

'The Lifted Veil' was the first work published by George Eliot after her identity had become generally known. It is the first work, therefore, in which the male voice is declaredly fictional. Now the authorial origin is no longer private, but in this text she finds another method of disguise: the absent author is obliterated behind the narrative figure, Latimer. This male growth from female plant is etiolated and spent. The tale constitutes her farewell to masculine voice. Latimer can see into everybody except the woman he marries.

'The Lifted Veil', like *Silas Marner* a year or two later, interrupts and delays a major enterprise. In one case, the writing of *The Mill on the Floss*, in the other, *Romola*. Such interruption is a phenomenon that many writers experience, and figures itself as a passionate and secret infatuation with an alternative imagination, which works under cover of a major project, delaying it, or, very occasionally, ousting it entirely. Its writing is complicit with dream.

The need for concealment was strong in George Eliot's creativity, though she distrusted it, indeed dreaded the speed with which it became deceit and enclosure. The new story registered this dread and also exorcised it. 'The Lifted Veil' was written in the midst of preparing her account of Maggie's education, where she describes also the equally falsifying education of a boy. In Tom Tulliver, she studied the hardening effects of an inappropriate classical education for a boy with practical talents and showed the stultification of his sensibility by St Ogg's ideas of 'manliness'. In Latimer, she presents an inverse picture: a boy full of sensitivity, longing for arts and literature, but force-fed with practical science, turned in upon himself by his own sense of debility. It is impossible for him ever to correspond to society's notion of a man, with his heightened imagination and 'half-womanish, half-ghostly beauty'. Caught across gender, he identifies himself intensely with his lost mother: 'even now, after the dreary lapse of long years, a slight trace of sensation accompanies the remembrance of her caress as she held me on her knee' ('The Lifted Veil', p. 280). He goes to Geneva and rows solitary on the lake (the allusions to Jean-Jacques Rousseau here are manifest), but unlike Rousseau he has 'the poet's sensibility without his voice'. He is obliterated, silent, consumed with a 'dumb passion'. He images the dread of inertia which beset George Eliot too. Latimer is afflicted with two kinds of preternatural vision—'preternatural', that favourite term of praise for writing which George Eliot admired. Having no means of expression, his vision drives inward and leaps outward. He sees into people's subconsciousness, and in flashes he foresees fixed images of the future. Like Macarthy's nightmare sympathy, this figure is burdened with the novelist's double power of authoritative analysis and prediction; he cannot escape his own insight nor give it any issue.

He manifests the dilemma that, however much the writer may eschew omniscience, it is not possible to be rid of prevision. He marries Bertha because she is the only person whose consciousness is impenetrable to him. She is the eeriest of the terrible water-nixies, female creatures without souls, who haunt George Eliot's work. And in the fight to the death between this married pair, Latimer and Bertha, George Eliot pits the terrors of imagination and of emptiness against each other. Latimer is bound in the knot of his own narrative, a narrative which, as Coleridge said narrative should, describes the ancient sexual symbol of the snake with its tail in its mouth. Latimer foresees his own death on the first page and reaches it on the last. The 'I' of the narrative and the 'double consciousness' of the narrator, the fear of never finding a voice, the fear that insight and sympathy will uncover only meanness, and that once the tawdry humdrum skin is penetrated it will reveal only the tawdry and the humdrum—these are all fears within George Eliot's creativity as she moves into a much more openly personal phase of her writing. Now she must find a stable address no longer facetiously playing upon masculine traits and concealing femaleness. Latimer, Tom and Maggie all represent the damage done to identity by education and by demands that the child polarise sexually and exclude those characteristics denied by society's preconceptions about the capabilities of men and women.

Chapter Four

# 'The Dark Woman Triumphs': Passion in *The Mill on the Floss*

## *I*

*The Mill on the Floss* first raises in an acute form the besetting problem to which George Eliot constantly returns. Is the only form of heroism open to women to be martyrdom? And should women accept that form of heroism at all? Heroism in literature is represented in many forms for men, martyrdom among them. But for women martyrdom has been the most powerful single channel for narrative activity and narrative conclusion. In *Clarissa* we have the most extensive form of the paradox. Clarissa's sensibility is accorded an extraordinary range and complexity. Her values impress the values of the narrative. The text is 'lisible' only by means of an accord between reader and the figure of Clarissa. Despite our frequent treacherous complicity with Lovelace, our pleasure in his insights and stratagems, our reading can find repose only by recourse to the writing of Clarissa, whose own discourse is whole, not fractured, not polymorphic, though constantly opposed and interrupted by the events and counter-events of other people's letters. It is this wholeness, this integrity, which conducts her towards martyrdom. Lovelace never makes choices; he doubles them. When she makes choices, she renounces other possibilities. So the text, as labyrinth, apes the form of Lovelace; the text as consequential sequence requires the presence—and the sacrifice—of Clarissa. As the book proceeds, more and more choices are fictitiously presented to her by the activities of Lovelace. These dream-choices, fictive possibilities, brush past her without impinging on her real situation, which is that of enclosure, resistance and isolation. She attempts escape and is brought back. She is surrounded by the treachery of other women. Even Anna Howe for a time misunderstands and abandons her. She is raped. She survives. 'Clarissa lives.' Her integrity, it proves, does not only rely upon her physical intactness. And yet she is elected to die. One by one the choices are closed down around her. She does not marry Lovelace. She does not retire to the country to manage in independence the estate left to her by her grandfather, a solution which Victorian women writers came to favour, as we have seen. Instead she organises her own death, writing her letters upon her coffin, in an epigrammatic domestication of her dilemma and her solution. She will claim death. Or Richardson will claim it for her.

Many of his women correspondents protested against the process of foreclosing which they saw happening. They tried to save her from his sacrificial act. He used his authority as author, originator, patriarch, to bring her—with infinite compunction—to death. Was he offering a critique of the current social order which made no space for women like Clarissa? Was he saving her for himself? Was he claiming for her the only form of epic action open to women—a sacrificial epic in which the woman, like Lucrece, sustains her integrity by self-immolation? He divests Clarissa's death of all suggestion of punishment. It is a Christ-like sacrifice, but, unlike Christ, it does not redeem. It demonstrates.

Perhaps it is worth noting that George Eliot seems to have appreciated *Sir Charles Grandison* more than *Clarissa*, and found its women's witty capacity for survival more pleasurable than Clarissa's long renunciation and assertion of the will. But that does not at all mean that she was less affected by *Clarissa*. (I shall argue a particular connection in the chapter on *Daniel Deronda*.) She resists its allurements precisely because they are so alluring to her. Of her heroines, only one, Maggie, shares Clarissa's fate—and then in the tumult of accident rather than as sustained choice. So Maggie may have her release and her fulfilment without being implicated in the will to death. That is not to say, however, that she is exempted from the will to martyrdom.

George Eliot found it necessary to distinguish between renunciation and martyrdom. Her men are inclined to accuse women of a will to martyrdom when what they are observing is a will to independence. In a social order which constrains women, of course, the desire for independence and for martyrdom may prove to have indistinguishable consequences, but they are not indistinguishable in their natures. The reality of choice is crucial in George Eliot's work. People frequently make choices before they have observed it (as Lydgate does in his impulse to comfort Rosamond which results in his engagement). But they recognise choice, even if retrospectively. What are the areas of choice open to women?

In a long review of George Eliot's career up to 1863,

'The Dark Woman Triumphs': Passion in *The Mill on the Floss*

Richard Simpson argues that

> The antithesis of passion and duty figures itself to her mind as a kind of sexual distinction; so that if woman could be defecated from all male fibres, she would be all passion, as man, purged of all feminine qualities, would be all hard duty. (Carroll, 1971, p.239)

He then neatly turns the screw of this argument a round further:

> It is natural that the authoress should make her women act male parts, and give her men something of a feminine character. Though she ought to be able to draw woman in herself, for the simple reason that she is a woman, yet she may be too far separated from the ordinary life of her sex to be a good judge of its relations. The direct power and the celebrity of authorship may obscure and replace the indirect influence and calm happiness of domestic feminine life . . . . Having thus taken up the male position, the male ideal becomes hers,—the ideal of power,—which, interpreted by her feminine heart and intellect, means the supremacy of passion in the affairs of the world. (Ibid, p.241)

Simpson shares the wearisome assumption that men can naturally portray women but not women men. However, the fear that she might have separated herself too far from the ordinary is one which George Eliot saw as the special difficulty of the woman artist, as we shall see in 'Armgart', and again in *Daniel Deronda*. Simpson here contrives to blame her both for being tainted with masculinity and femininity. Nevertheless, the point he makes about the *power* of the author is not one to be passed over lightly. By claiming 'the male position' (what he elsewhere calls 'direct power through reasoning and speech') she has, according to his analysis, forfeited contact with the actual social condition of women. 'She gives us her view of woman's vocation, and paints things as they ought to be, not as they are.' Such criticism may help to account for the greater emphasis on typicality in the ordering of women in her late novels. No one after Maggie is allowed to issue out of her condition.

Many Victorian commentators characterised George Eliot as a novelist preoccupied with passion. If we identify passion solely with sexual love between peers we shall find a dearth of any extended description of such love-sensation in her work. Henry James commented on the singular austerity with which George Eliot treated love, suggesting that *Middlemarch* and *Daniel Deronda* did

> seem to foreign readers, probably, like vast, cold, commodious, respectable rooms, through whose window-panes one sees a snow-covered landscape, and across whose acres of sober-hued carpet one looks in vain for a fireplace or a fire. (James, 1878, p.219)

It is necessary to insist, in our culture, that passion does not describe solely heterosexual love-affairs. If her representations of sexual encounter are at the opposite extreme of reticence from *My Secret Life*, it is worth remembering Foucault's comment that that work is part of the Victorian process of transforming sex into discourse. But if we understand passion in relationships as vehement human need sustained past the accomplishment of moments of desire, we shall more exactly mark what it meant for her.

A French critic in the 1870s, remarked that her writing was 'très éloquent dans la peinture du remords, beaucoup moins animé pourtant quand il s'agit d'exprimer l'amour.' This pinpoints exactly one of the human passions that she most fully understood: the obsessional reliving of the spent moment in an attempt to make it change its shape, to escape its shame and regret. Remorse is one of the most engrossing emotions for narrative, since it strives to recuperate a bearable reading, its obsessional repetition seeking to be rid of the need yet again to retell the same fixed story. George Eliot was able both through the organisation of repetition and through the analysis of its glaring fixity of recall to explore the passionate experience of remorse. Indeed, in *Daniel Deronda*, Gwendolen's self-discovery is fuelled almost entirely by remorse.

In Maggie, passion takes the form of vehement intellectual need experienced as emotion. Desire for knowledge, for 'more instruments playing together', had traditionally been enregistered as the man's story. Faust and his wild passion for full possession of the world that knowledge may open, is saved by the innocent, stay-at-home, untutored Gretchen. Steadfast love is divided from the thirst for knowledge, polarised as female and male. George Eliot rejects that polarisation, first in Maggie, and then, more and more powerfully in the later novels by means of the polymathic narrative which, through learning, constantly discovers emotional connection. The writing ranges freely through and beyond such oppositions, but it also experiences them. In 'Armgart' we are presented with the urgency of creative anger and need—an anger which is generated more by desire than by frustration, and a desire which is for the creative act itself:

> I carry my revenges in my throat;
> I love in singing, and am loved again.
> *(Poems*, p.175)

Several feminist critics, notably Christ (1976) and Midler (1980), have pointed out the urgency of anger in George

Eliot's creativity and her need, also, to reach beyond anger. In her anger, although there is often an edge of frustration and criticism of current social forms, there is frequently also a more Pythian 'rage'. Not all anger is social reformist nor seeking solution.

Charlotte Brontë shows the same phenomenon in a more pronounced form. Contemporary critics were to some extent at a loss to describe what they found so disturbing in her work. The *Blackwood's* reviewer set it alongside seditious acts and European revolt. The surging vehemence of *claim* subverted steady forms. And we find this claim in the activity of telling, as well as in what is told. Writing, making, publishing, are all claims to space and attention. The form of first person in *Jane Eyre*, and the centrality of Maggie's intellectual growth in *The Mill*, assert the importance of unregarded life. They make us *recognise* that life. George Eliot's special attention is given to 'unhistoric acts' and to individual lives without national importance. She shows such lives and such acts as being embroiled in movements recognisable from history books. She raises the unregarded into significance. Her use of double time-schemes in all her works except *Daniel Deronda* means that the reader is required not only to recognise the past but to appraise the present in a carefully experimental series of relations to the past.

Elaine Showalter (1977) sees the story of Maggie Tulliver as George Eliot's concession to a particularly Victorian configuration of the female which produces a 'passive, self-destructive heroine'. This reading makes Maggie sound more renunciatory than she is portrayed as being in the book. As Nina Auerbach (1982) shows, Maggie is connected from the beginning of the story with the demonic.

> 'Oh I'll tell you what that means. It's a dreadful picture, isn't it? But I can't help looking at it. That old woman in the water's a witch—they've put her in to find out whether she's a witch or no, and if she swims she's a witch, if she's drowned—and killed, you know—she's innocent, and not a witch, but only a poor silly old woman. But what good would it do her then, you know, when she was drowned? Only, I suppose, she'd go to heaven, and God would make it up to her.' (*The Mill*, I, p.21, Bk.I, ch.3)

Maggie here cites the tale of the witch in Defoe's *History of the Devil*. The witch epitomises Maggie's bind. If she is innocent, she drowns. If she bobs up again, she is guilty. Is Maggie's drowning used in some half-magical way to prove her innocence? If so, such innocence is useless. Like the witch, Maggie is dead. Only the narrator can 'make it up to her'. The last chapter, indeed, is entitled 'The Final Rescue', and that rescue is undertaken by the writer. Within the work, Maggie herself makes jokes about another such magical ordering in novels and fairy-tales, that of the blond and the dark heroine. The blond represents restraint and social order, the dark, passion and disruption. The blond is bound to win, and Maggie resents that. So do we. Lucy sees Maggie's learning as 'witchcraft': 'part of your general uncanniness' (II, p.187, Bk.VI, ch.3).

> 'I didn't finish the book,' said Maggie. 'As soon as I came to the blond-haired young lady reading in the park, I shut it up, and determined to read no further. I foresaw that that light-complexioned girl would win away all the love from Corinne and make her miserable. I'm determined to read no more books where the blond-haired women carry away all the happiness. I should begin to have a prejudice against them. If you could give me some story, now, where the dark woman triumphs, it would restore the balance. I want to

avenge Rebecca and Flora MacIvor, and Minna and all the rest of the dark unhappy ones.' (II, p.102, Bk.V, Ch.4)

The work playfully draws attention to its own order and knowingly prognosticates what comes to seem inevitable: Maggie's defeat. Yet it presages, too, the paradoxical sense of Maggie's triumph and vengeance with which, despite her death, the book concludes.

The novel is full of meaning glimpsed from earlier literature. Maggie is determinedly shut out by the education system, with its stereotypes of male and female, from classical learning, though she demonstrates her readiness and skill at Mr Stelling's house (Jacobus, 1981, pp. 207–22). But the magical fragmentariness also feeds her:

> She presently made up her mind to skip the rules in the Syntax—the examples became so absorbing. The mysterious sentences, snatched from an unknown context,—like strange horns of beasts, and leaves of unknown plants, brought from some far-off region—gave boundless scope to her imagination, and were all the more fascinating because they were in a peculiar tongue of their own, which she could learn to interpret. (I, p.228, Bk.II, ch.1)

Both Tom and Maggie, for differing reasons, are dependent on Philip, the wounded Philoctetes, to give them access to the warmth of learning in their lives. The roused meaning of flat text needs a speaking voice to make it heard. Learning can enter their youth as story:

> He listened with great interest to a new story of Philip's about a man who had a very bad wound in his foot, and cried out so dreadfully with the pain that his friends could bear with him no longer, but put him ashore on a desert island, with nothing but some wonderful poisoned arrows to kill animals with for food.

> 'I didn't roar out a bit, you know,' Tom said, 'and I daresay my foot was as bad as his. It's cowardly to roar.'
>
> But Maggie would have it that when anything hurt you very much, it was quite permissible to cry out, and it was cruel of people not to bear it. She wanted to know if Philoctetes had a sister, and why *she* didn't go with him on the desert island and take care of him. (I, pp.285-6, Bk.II, ch.6)

These stories are shared complicitly by author and reader, weaving connections not always apparent to those within the text. Like metaphor, they allow meaning to emerge without settling. And yet George Eliot will not allow the reader to remain comfortable within the possession of these connections: 'light irony' and easy cultural pretensions may be bought dear, and Maggie's 'false quantities' go with a deeper learning than Tom's.

> Now and then, that sort of enthusiasm finds a far-echoing voice that comes from an experience springing out of the deepest need. And it was by being brought within the long lingering vibrations of such a voice that Maggie, with her girl's face and unnoted sorrows, found an effort and a hope that helped her through years of loneliness, making out a faith for herself without the aid of established authorities and appointed guides—for they were not at hand, and her need was pressing. (II, p.38, Bk.IV, ch.3)

Thomas à Kempis's *Imitation of Christ* speaks to Maggie as voice, in a way that is made to sustain the emphasis of the address to the reader immediately afterwards.

> But good society, floated on gossamer wings of light irony, is of very expensive production; requiring nothing less than a wide and arduous national life condensed in unfragrant deafening factories, cramping itself in mines, sweating at

furnaces, grinding, hammering, weaving under more or less oppression of carbonic acid—or else, spread over sheep-walks, and scattered in lonely houses and huts on the clayey or chalky corn-lands, where the rainy days look dreary. This wide national life is based entirely on emphasis—the emphasis of want. (II, p.37, Bk.IV, ch. 3)

Philip says of himself ' "my voice is middling—like everything else in me".' But Philip is the interpreter, a redeemed version of Latimer, able despite his physical debility to see precisely and kindly into the sensibility of others. He is kind, in some ways more kind or 'kinned' to Maggie than her brother, though in the end it is blood-bond and primitive memory that hold her. His exclusion from active life sets him alongside Maggie in a way which confuses likeness and difference. He tempts Maggie with his offer to be 'brother and teacher', but he can never satisfy her sexually.

For Maggie, there can be no accommodation with society, because the community in which she has grown up, and the culture of which this is an expression, will accord her nature no recognition.

'Girls can't do Euclid: can they, sir?'
'They can pick up a little of everything, I daresay,' said Mr Stelling. 'They've a great deal of superficial cleverness; but they couldn't go far into anything. They're quick and shallow.' . . . As for Maggie, she had hardly ever been so mortified. She had been so proud to be called 'quick' all her little life, and now it appeared that this quickness was the brand of inferiority. (I, pp.232–3, Bk.II, ch.1)

She is one of the aberrations of breeding:

'An' a pleasant sort o' soft woman may go on breeding you stupid lads and cute wenches, till it's like as if the world was turned topsy-turvy.' (I, p.24, Bk.I, ch.3)

She resists bonding herself to other women, because they represent so much she must gainsay.

> 'I think all women are crosser than men,' said Maggie. 'Aunt Glegg's a great deal crosser than Uncle Glegg, and mother scolds me more than father does.'
>
> 'Well, *you'll* be a woman some day,' said Tom, 'so *you* needn't talk.'
>
> 'But I shall be a *clever* woman,' said Maggie, with a toss.
>
> 'Oh, I daresay, and a nasty conceited thing. Everybody'll hate you.' (I, p.226, Bk.II, ch.1)

The work excels at taut humour which catches the sound of women gossiping, pinched into the forms of their narrow society. The aunts with cheerful gloom give voice to the domestic powers and repression of St Ogg's.

Maggie's other favourite childhood reading, *Pilgrim's Progress*, is a story of tribulations ending in triumph and delight. Loved as that model is, it is also eschewed, though something of its mood of triumphal reconcilement is retained. Like Christian, Maggie and Tom go down into the river. Through careful, humanistic negatives, George Eliot allows a secular faith in human accord to predict this final scene:

> there was an undefined sense of reconcilement with her brother: what quarrel, what harshness, what unbelief in each other can subsist in the presence of a great calamity, when all the artificial vesture of our life is gone, and we are all one with another in primitive mortal needs? (II, p.395, Bk.VII, ch.5)

The book refuses to consider the question: how long can that oneness survive after calamity?—unless Tom and Maggie's immediate death implies a dour answer.

The brother–sister relationship had a particular significance for George Eliot. There were literary-historical as well as biographical reasons for its power. She came a generation after the Romantic writers, and in particular her much reverenced Wordsworth, had made of the relationship an epipsychidion: a marriage of the soul with itself, the yolk and white of Plato's parable. George Eliot's intense childhood relationship with her brother, always perhaps more intense on her side than his, and their complete rupture after she went to live with Lewes, form a complete and punctuated story on which, painfully, she continued to look back.

In narrative terms, the *containment* of the relationship within the period of her youth intensified its meaning. The identification of brother and sister and their subsequent rupture, created powerful metaphors for the growth of identity, which, in a just pre-Freudian age, could provide a symbolic discourse capable of analysing the Deronda–Gwendolen relationship as much as the Tom–Maggie relationship.

Antigone, her significant heroine, who stood against the authority of state and king, indeflectable, endured all to give her brother proper burial. Foucault writes in *The History of Sexuality*, I,

> When a long while ago the West discovered love, it bestowed on it a value high enough to make death acceptable; nowadays it is sex that claims this equivalence, the highest of all, . . . the fictitious point of sex . . . exerts enough charm on everyone for them to accept hearing the grumble of death within it. (Foucault, 1979, p.156)

In the story of Antigone, love, duty, kinship, passion and death grumble within one another. Sex is, in one sense, excluded. Yet through Antigone's passional commitment, erotic emotion permeates the story. Perhaps, too, we should pay attention to her desired act: to give her brother proper burial, to lay him to rest. To honour him and to be free of him. In the Antigone story, the consequence is that the heroine is buried alive. Maggie Tulliver drowns alongside Tom. But George Eliot survived after Marian Evans' alienation from her brother—was even born out of that alienation.

## II

It would not suffice to provide a critique of *The Mill* in terms of the social realism that its conclusion outfaces. The opening equally with the ending disturbs sociological description. The book is enclosed within a preliminary dream, in which an unsexed narrator gradually converts a present so immediate that it seems at first to lack even verb, back into a warmed but vitiated past. The book opens with this sentence:

> A wide plain, where the broadening Floss hurries on between its green banks to the sea, and the loving tide, rushing to meet it, checks its passage with an impetuous embrace. (I, p.3, Bk.I, ch.1)

The passional sweep, the lack of preliminaries, makes for an effusiveness in that first description which is both embarrassing and opening. The reader resists, and is swept along, is met by the verb 'checks', whose sense gives way into impetuous embrace. What is described is dilemma: the downward hurrying river met by the in-rushing tide: the moment of arrest and embrace is emphasised, just before permeation. We do not know, since this is the opening, at what scope to read. We slide between scales. Then, the eroticism of the opening sentence is yoked back into economic order,

> the black ships—laden with the fresh-scented fir-planks, with rounded sacks of oil-bearing seed, or with the dark-glitter of coal—are borne along to the town of St Ogg's. (I, p.3, Bk.I, ch.1)

The senses (scent, touch, sight) are engaged and the second paragraph ends with the description of the mill-stream:

> The stream is brimful now, and lies high in this withy plantation, and half drowns the grassy fringe of the croft .... As I look at the full stream, the vivid grass, the delicate bright-green powder softening the outline of the great trunks and branches that gleam from under the bare purple boughs, I am in love with moistness. (I, p.4, Bk.I, ch.1)

The knowledge of a seeing eye is brought close through touch: 'I am in love with moistness.' The bodily intimacy of a fully-known landscape, body-scape, is voiced in the first person. Plenitude is now. The writer twice recurs to that metaphor of creative deafness which we have examined in the tale of Parizade, once, in the quirky anthropomorphism of the little river's 'low placid voice, the voice of one who is deaf and loving', and, again, in the mill-stream:

> The rush of the water, and the booming of the mill, bring a dreamy deafness, which seems to heighten the peacefulness of the scene. They are like a great curtain of sound, shutting one out from the world beyond. (I, p.5, Bk.I, ch.1)

Enclosure in another's dream—the creation of meta-memory—is the project here. And that deep drop into irrecoverable intimacy preludes our reading of the text. In 'The Lifted Veil', written soon after beginning *The Mill*, the entry into another's consciousness is combined with a recoil of memory which is threatening and arid. The first person here in *The Mill* is uncharacterised, and the end of the chapter has an awkward innocence of narrative technique about it, a plangent archness like that of Charles Lamb in 'Dream Children'. As so often with first person in George Eliot, the figure suggested is passive, here poised on the verge of maleness.

The opening, forgotten as we read on, has 'left its trace, and lives in us still', though 'blent irrecoverably' with later impressions in the text. The description of the river in the opening sentence is taken over into descriptions of Maggie's behaviour: 'Maggie rushed to her deeds with passionate impulse' or

> For poor little Maggie had at once the timidity of an active imagination, and the daring that comes from overmastering impulse. She had rushed into the adventure of seeking her unknown kindred, the gypsies. (I, p.164, Bk.I, ch.11)

At the end of the book the 'dream-like' action of the flooded river re-enters the narrative, taking with it Maggie who has lived alongside it, played by it and sometimes been identified with it. She has been threatened with drowning for her mischief with the water and has floated away with Stephen in the drift of need and desire. Finally, the two currents of river and tide meet and lock in the death-embrace of Tom and Maggie.

Perhaps it is exactly the assuaging of desire which is unsatisfying at the end. It is Maggie's flood, 'uncannily' approaching to drown and rescue her. Throughout the

book a sense of the 'uncanniness' of inner life and the
recalcitrance of outward circumstance have been equally
maintained. In this book 'tide' and 'tidings', both
insistent words, have kept each to its own domain of
natural energy and narrative. But at the end they are
confused.

Desire in this society cannot be satisfied. Maggie gives
expression to desires which cannot be contained in any
of the social forms available:' "I was never satisfied with
a *little* of anything",' she says to Philip, in renouncing
him,

> 'That is why it is better for me to do without earthly
> happiness altogether . . . . I never felt that I had enough
> music—I wanted more instruments playing together—I
> wanted voices to be fuller and deeper.' (II, p.95, Bk.V, ch.3)

It is this expression of female desire, the desire for
knowledge, for sexual love, for free life, which is the
unremitting narrative urgency of *The Mill on the Floss*, a
desire for new forms of life unrealisable in terms of the
old order and the fixed stereotypes by which she is
surrounded. The desires (for knowledge, sexual love,
freedom) are not different from those of men; the
difference is in the breaking of the taboo on them, the
claiming of them as female desires.

But the work is also combative towards its heroine.
She is unremittingly tested, despite those guard words
such as 'poor Maggie', 'poor child', which seem to offer
her shelter. The intimacy and the unremittingness
together create the particular tonic insight of the work;
it becomes implacably opposed to half-measures. It is in
these terms, also, that the ending is best understood.
Maggie drowns. She sloughs off compromise. The
narrative finally rejects the form of *Bildungsroman*, in
which the growing ego of a young man comes to terms

with the society in which it dwells and accepts both attrition and continuity. Maggie's *Bildung* takes her only to the point where she knows that there is no place for her in her own community, since she has rowed away with Stephen and returned not married to him. All would have been forgiven in time if they had married. But her individualistic insistence on old attachments, not on social forms, puts her irrevocably at odds with the codes by which her community is conditioned, despite their lip-service to kinship. In George Eliot's later books aggression, anger and frustration become more openly menacing energies, expressed in narrative as well as persons. In *The Mill on the Floss* Maggie's anger finds it very difficult to place itself without threatening her most deeply needed relationships (with Tom, with her father). So it recoils upon herself. She internalises it as self-doubt and inadequacy. Passionate feeling and passionate knowledge must both be *grown out of* if she is to survive in her environment.

Her swollen trouble, the outrage which cannot be countenanced as self-assertion, at the end of the book is naturalised as flood. In that way she cannot be held responsible for it. The sense of Maggie ceasing to be responsible, of her being freed from the inevitability of the social constraint and contract to which she has subdued herself, must trouble readers. Her heart's desire—the return to childhood, erotic reunion with her brother, the knitting up again of the divided self which has been split into the twin forms of male and female each with their separate order: these are desires which it is given to all to feel and none to fulfil. That is why she must die: she has refused Stephen *Guest*, the fleeting displacement of an older desire, as his name suggests.

The level of desire explored at the end of the book is *a-historical*, and ceases to be focused as a criticism of a specific social order. Up to that point, when it seemed that Maggie must endure attrition, misunderstanding, the drudging work of being a governess, the mode of the novel has been that of social critique: a recognition of the grinding power of social mores which are *capable of being changed*. Maggie's release removes the question of social change. Society's treatment of her is first brought into question, and then the question is set aside.

Floods may happen. The flooding river is part of the natural conditions which have produced the particular economic order of St. Ogg's. The flood thus has meanings which pull in opposing directions: outside the social and yet within economic order, there is always the possibility of uncontrollable natural event which comes willy-nilly and must takes its course. At the same time, the analogy with sexual passion is strong, and particularly with female passion. Among the seventeenth-century musicians and lyricists whom Maggie admires such imagery is common:

> Weep, O mine eyes, and cease not:
> Your spring-tides, alas, methinks increase not,
> O when, O when begin you
> To swell so high that I may drown me in you?

So, as individual and as sexual symbol, the flood is Maggie's. 'She was not bewildered for an instant—she knew it was the flood.' The Floss has been persistently connected with the re-awakening of her desire:

> And beyond, the silvery breadth of the dear old Floss . . . Maggie's eye began to fill with tears . . . . Memory and imagination urged upon her a sense of privation too keen to let her taste what was offered in the transient present: her future, she thought, was likely to be worse than her past, for after her years of contented renunciation, she had

slipped back into desire and longing. (II, pp.166-7, Bk.VI, ch.2)

But the Floss is also connected with memory as admonition: 'If the past is not to bind us, where can duty lie?' She had floated downstream with Stephen. Now the flood removes the confines of stream: 'There was no choice of courses, no room for hesitation, and she floated into the current' 'Swiftly she went now, without effort' (Book VII, p.396).

The freedom that Maggie is offered is the removal of choice. She had made the utmost effort of choice and of will in renouncing Stephen. She had chosen martyrdom. Now choice is no longer demanded of her. She can float with the current. And the current restores her to 'primitive mortal needs':

> the strong resurgent love towards her brother that swept away all the later impressions of hard, cruel offence and misunderstanding, and left only the deep, underlying, unshakeable memories of early union (II, p.395, Bk. VII, ch.5),

a union which is realised in the death-embrace: 'brother and sister had gone down in an embrace never to be parted' (II, p.400, Bk.VII, ch.5).

This *liebestod*, the consummation of a union for which there is no place in the social order, is a deeper psychic challenge to the reader than the repudiated union with Stephen—a union which, though outside marriage, mimics parallel social forms. In the union of Maggie and Tom there is both the fullness of incestuous love, and a claim for a profound reconstitution of the self as split between the permitted potentialities of male and female. The knitting-up is an acceptance of male and female, which in education are estranged into socialised gender

101

roles. Otto Rank suggests of the Oedipus myth that incest is a symbol of man's 'self-creative urge' (Rank, 1914). And here, lateral incest, the twinning and recombination of opposed selves, may be the expression of another 'self-creative urge'.

But it is an acceptance which can find its form and moment only in death. It is not envisaged as a part of life. It is summation, but it also expresses nostalgia for an earlier world here cleansed of its complexity. Within the novel we have *not* much seen Maggie and Tom in childhood with their little hands clasped in love, roaming the daisied fields together. There is only one episode where he is not cross or domineering towards her. We have seen them at odds, awkwardly fond, never finding quite how to fit together, tugging apart in their individual needs.

The end of the book sets up double-binds of the kind that Maggie had observed much earlier when in her early childhood she read Defoe's *History of the Devil* and embarrassed her father with her improper knowledge of the way the world treats women whom it selects as deviants. At the end of *The Mill on the Floss*, Maggie drowns, and is innocent, and receives her reward momentously and in an unsustainable instant in this world. She has rowed safely back to the mill. Tom, seeing the 'huge fragments, clinging together in fatal fellowship' approaching them, reacts thus: ' "It is coming, Maggie!" Tom said, in a deep hoarse voice, loosing the oars, and clasping her' (II, p.400, Bk.VII, ch.5).

The orgasmic reference is overwhelming, and overwhelms them: and so does the flood. The transgressions that George Eliot liberates at the end of the novel are in that same moment suppressed and done away with. Opposing forces appear not in the calm of enigma but in the vehemence of conclusion. Conclusion permits events without consequences and without social force.

Lawrence ironises this episode in *Women in Love* by removing it from its privileged position as conclusion, and transferring blame to the female, turning it back into an image of the male entrapped. In George Eliot both man and woman are freed from that need to *blame* which, increasingly, she recognises in her writing and which the writing makes the reader recognise in herself and himself. But here she has not yet found a way of removing blame without removing consequences. By this I mean that the end of *The Mill on the Floss* cannot quite sustain both social enquiry and individual need.

Much later in her life, George Eliot, commenting on the social parallels between fiction and the conditions which produced her creative memories remarked to Emily Davies that things were worse in that society than she had shown them in the novel: 'She considers that in *The Mill on the Floss*, everything is softened, as compared with real life. Her own experience she said was worse' (Haight, 1978, 8, p.465).

In the same conversation, using (if Emily Davies correctly recollects the metaphorical terms) images which draw on the terms of the novel, she said that her purpose in writing it

> was to show the conflict which is going on everywhere when the young generation with its higher culture comes into collision with the older, and in which, she said, so many young hearts make shipwreck far worse than Maggie.

That conversation took place while she was writing *Middlemarch*, which itself continues to examine the curtailing conditions which chafe the young into seeking freer forms for experience and activity. In *Middlemarch* there is no ready escape route, no naturalisation of *thanatos* as a feasible liberation from the demands of ordinary existence. The subversive vehemence of Maggie's fate both releases from the bounds of social realism and yet neutralises its own commentary by allowing her (and so us) the plenitude which is nowhere available within her society.

Ruskin, writing after George Eliot's death in 1881 fulminates against the ordinariness of the people in *The Mill* and sees them as valueless because typical:

> There is not a single person in the book of the smallest importance to anybody in the world but themselves, or whose qualities deserved so much as a line of printer's type in their description. There is no girl alive, fairly clever, half educated, and unluckily related, whose life has not at least as much in it as Maggie's, to be described and to be pitied . . . while the rest of the characters are simply the sweepings out of a Pentonville omnibus. (Carroll, 1971, p.167)

To George Eliot, they were valuable *because* typical, because they could stand for many others besides themselves. For other girls alive and other boys, whose situation is not usually described or pitied. Tom, as George Eliot insists, is as much a victim of rigid stereotyping as is Maggie. His schooling might have suited Maggie, frustrated with lack of learning, but stultifies Tom. On Tom falls the full weight of required manliness, sealing him into a pig-headed dutifulness and burdening him too young with certainty.

Richard Jenkyn comments on George Eliot's counter-creed to that of Greek tragedy: 'The phrase *ti megethos* a "certain largeness" [which Maggie's small child action of pushing Lucy in the mud lacks] . . . is taken from Aristotle, who argued that the action of a tragedy had to have a certain greatness or grandeur to it. George Eliot rejects this view' (Jenkyn, 1980, pp.118–19). But 'a certain largeness' *is* required and created: the largeness of the reader's awakened consciousness, which, sustained by the writing, becomes capable of taking the full measure of things.

Dinah Mulock, the author of *John Halifax, Gentleman*, (1857), in the course of a perceptive review shaped by her own religious preoccupations, is troubled specifically by this problem of typicality:

> In the whole history of this fascinating *Maggie* there is a picturesque piteousness which somehow confuses one's sense of right and wrong. Yet what . . . is to become of the hundreds of clever girls, born of uncongenial parents, hemmed in with unsympathising kindred of the Dodson sort, blest with no lover on whom to bestow their strong affections, no friend to whom to cling for guidance and support? They must fight their way, heaven help them! alone and unaided, through cloud and darkness, to the light. And, thank heaven, hundreds of them do, and live to hold out a helping hand afterwards to thousands more. (Carroll, 1971, p.157)

Maggie's fate, 'death, welcomed as the solution to all difficulties, the escape from all pain', troubles Dinah Mulock because it reneges on endurance and companionship—the parallel troubles between the girl in the writing and the girls in the world. She objects to Maggie's escape more than to her conduct. In that, she was rare.

The recoil both from the possibility of Maggie's love for Stephen and from what was seen as the sensuality of George Eliot's writing is a more common response. One reviewer, in particular, feels with a physical shudder the impropriety of conjuring the sensations of the opposite sex:

But there is a kind of love-making which seems to possess a strange fascination for the modern female novelist. Currer Bell and George Eliot, and we may add George Sand, all like to dwell on love as a strange overmastering force which, through the senses, captivates and enthrals the soul. They linger on the description of the physical sensations that accompany the meeting of hearts of love. Curiously, too, they all like to describe these sensations as they conceive them to exist in men. We are bound to say that their conceptions are true and adequate. But we are not sure that it is quite consistent with feminine delicacy to lay so much stress on the bodily feelings of the other sex . . . . [and] In points like these, it may be observed that men are more delicate than women. There are very few men who would not shrink from putting into words what they might imagine to be the physical effects of love in a woman. (Carroll, 1971, pp.118–19)

This prurient delicacy, the fear of representing, or of *feeling* what the other sex may feel, sees the woman writer's entry into masculine sensation as a violation of woman's delicacy (and an invasion of the club). The stereotype of separate worlds is used to complain of the sensual description of Maggie's arm, and of Stephen covering it with kisses—a description which doubly affronts, written by a woman, making it plain that arousal crosses sexual difference. Had she represented only Maggie's inner sensations, all might have been well.

We can see in this debate the extent to which George Eliot challenged the boundaries of woman's role by her insistence that the woman novelist should not be confined to imaging women. She denied any exclusive bond between writer and her own sex, even while she acknowledged kinship. Edith Simcox's satisfyingly unexpected characterisation of George Eliot, or Marian Lewes, after her death, emphasises the passion in her nature, 'the fulness of life and loving energy that could not accept a lot of negations' (McKenzie, 1961, p.116).

The will to *have*, and not to stand aside, which informs her life beneath its slow surface, is present also in the writing's determination to enter discourse and knowledge attributed to both sexes. And it is there, too, in the narrative energy which sustains diverse possibilities and interactions. In this early book, as in *Scenes of Clerical Life*, the lyrical solution of death is accepted. But later, death never comes at the end of her narrative, at least for her women. They must go on living. The emphasis on laying alongside, on fugitive and sustained analogies between human lots, becomes a means of entering and knowing. Though renunciation is so often her topic, it is not her practice as a novelist.

Chapter Five

# Fostering Fictions: *Romola,*
# *Silas Marner, Felix Holt*

## *I*

In George Eliot's next four books the theme of genetic
parents and foster-parents becomes remarkably important. *Romola* and *Felix Holt* are, in differing degrees,
concerned with adultery and the children born of it,
while in *Silas Marner* there is a secret marriage and child.
*Romola* turns on Tito's rejection of his bond to his foster-
father. *The Spanish Gypsy* concerns the plight of Fedalma,
brought up among the Spanish nobility and reclaimed on
the eve of her marriage by her unknown father, the
gypsy chieftain, who is engaged in a guerilla war against
Spain. Romola and Silas Marner both become foster-
parents and this relationship brings about the satisfactory conclusion of the books. Rufus Lyon in *Felix Holt* is
another perfect foster-father who like the good foster-
father of Princess Parizade and her brothers 'attached
himself to them entirely; he watched over their rising
years with the solicitude of a real parent'—or more than

a real parent, as George Eliot observes the difficult practice of parenting in these novels. All three novels bring into the foreground the real and the 'fictional' nature of fathering.

This chapter will discuss the significance of mothers and of fathers, and consider the nature of the displacement involved in proposing a conflict between natural parents and nurturing parents. Within these oppositions what is the significance of the Madonna? For the novelist who, like George Eliot, sets so much store by sympathy, the chosen and unnatured bond of 'fostering' is crucial. Working with other people's language, other people's experience, being inhabited by their words—these are the conditions of creativity. What did the concept of the virgin mother mean for George Eliot? and why did it have so strong a symbolic power for her? What bearing does the privileged status of adoptive parents in her novels have on her own role as a writer of fiction? The power of the author to initiate, determine and condition is clearly one that George Eliot felt the need to mitigate. One notable metaphor by which she sought to explicate the extent of authorial control and textual freedom is that of motherhood:

> Exultation is a dream before achievement, and rarely comes after. What comes after, is rather the sense that the work has been produced within one, like offspring, developing and growing by some force of which one's own life has only served as a vehicle, and that what is left of oneself is only a poor husk. (Haight, 1978, VIII, p.383)

When Marian Evans went to live with Lewes she acquired a galaxy of new names: she had already been known among her friends as Pollyann, which she noted was close to Apollyon, Bunyan's devil, now she was also George Eliot, Marian Lewes, Polly, Madonna and

Mutter. Lewes's three sons, to whom she became a loving stepmother, called her by this last name. Stepmothers are notably absent figures in her fiction, though in the conditions of mother and child mortality among the Victorians they were common enough in Victorian society, and Elizabeth Gaskell, for example, gives a brilliant picture of the difficulties of the relationship in *Wives and Daughters*. But foster-fathers abound. This weakened form of the father figure, yearning with affection towards the female child he nurtures, may have had an element of wish-fulfilment for the author looking back on her own less demonstrative father. But such figures also set hard questions about kin and descent, and about the insistence on sustaining the hegemony of blood succession in landed society. They highlight and question the assumption that origins, fathers, law and descent have some rational connection.

One of Marian Evans' earliest references to the Madonna is caustic. She is imaged as a plaster figurine, in language which looks far forward to the relationship of Lydgate and Rosamond nearly thirty years later:

> Men pay a heavy price for their reluctance to encourage self-help and independent resources in women. The precious meridian years of many a man of genius have to be spent in the toil of routine, that an 'establishment' may be kept up for a woman who can understand none of his yearning, who is fit for nothing but to sit in her drawing room like a doll-Madonna in her shrine. (Pinney, 1963, pp.204–5)

In Weimar with Lewes in the 1850s she was so overcome by Raphael's Madonna that she felt almost hysterical. Late in her life she asked Edith Simcox not to call her mother. The figure of the virgin giving birth, becoming implicated in 'incarnate history', was one that fascinated her—and fascinated her not only morally but as an image of the problematical relationship of the artist to her creation. In her well-known letter to Harrison in 1866, she speaks of the problem of presenting characters as if they had first appeared to the writer bodily rather than conceptually. The idea of the woman, impregnated by idea and spirit, sharing with no bodily partner, making beings who are seen by others as her productions, her descendants, is one that seems to haunt George Eliot imaginatively and which she had to test rather than accept. She had avoided the ordinary lot of women. She had not herself become part of the world of descent, but she is persistently teased by the problem of parenting, of nurturing. She considers repeatedly the Virgin, occupied by another; the intact invaded, or fulfilled, by the maternal. She ebulliently, sometimes sentimentally, celebrates the joys of motherhood. She increasingly doubts them in her later work: she privileges nurture above nature. She caustically queries the conventional praise of motherhood in *Felix Holt*. She keeps children right on the periphery of *Middlemarch*. And in her final work, *Daniel Deronda*, the search for the mother becomes a binding theme; it is a search which can never be fulfilled but which at this stage of her career has entirely driven out the love-quest for the father which was the central practice of memory in *The Mill on the Floss*.

Bonnie Zimmerman, in her useful and interesting essay 'The Mother's History' argues that

> there are two categories of George Eliot heroines: the productive and the sterile . . . . Women who step beyond the social and biological limitations of womankind, who desire to transcend the ordinary 'lot of woman' by any means no

matter how admirable, who defy sexual standards, who rebel rather than submit; these women are visited with the curse of sterility. (Zimmerman, 1980, pp.82–3)

But is sterility shown as a curse? Is not that assumption merely stereotypical? Sometimes George Eliot seems, rather, to protect her heroines with fairy-tale ease against the curse of pregnancy within an unloving marriage. Women are not usually, outside books, protected from childbearing because all is not well in their marriage. George Eliot writes of a period before women could control their own fertility. The writer here controls it for them: Romola, Dorothea in her marriage to Casaubon, and Gwendolen are exempted from child-bearing. And the act of childbearing can hardly be seen as a reward, for Hetty, or for Molly in *Silas Marner*, or for Mrs Transome who carries the full brunt of the ideological burden. She bears first an idiot child to her unloved husband and then a blooming boy to the lover will will later coldly reject her. Or can Mrs Glasher (whose name 'glacier' is a transposition of Grandcourt's qualities rather than her own) be said to be in a *productive* situation, trapped with her four children in a house encroached on by coal-fields, at the mercy of Grand-court's fitful visits? It seems to me mistaken to identify motherhood with productivity. For example, productiv-ity, in the sense of producing change, is more notable in Dinah's preaching than in her marriage, which necessar-ily *ends* the book: there is no more to be said.

On the other hand, it is true that George Eliot only once shows us a thriving and independent 'old maid'. Indeed, there is an extraordinary absence of single women in her fiction, or even women living on their own. Again, the contrast with Elizabeth Gaskell or Charlotte Brontë focuses the point. In particular, we recall the opening of *Cranford*: 'In the first place, Cranford is in possession of the Amazons; all the holders of houses above a certain rent are women.' In George Eliot's work, Priscilla Lammeter in *Silas Marner* is the one example of a woman who has chosen fruitfully to live single, though, as she cheerfully admits, her independence relies on having 'fortn'. And she is claimed by Richard Simpson as an honorary man on account of the precision and regularity of her pork-pies:

> Priscilla Lammeter, the only old maid whom George Eliot attempts to describe, exhibits the manly character of her mind precisely in this 'My pork pies,' she says, 'don't turn out well by chance.' (Carroll, 1971, p.244)

Independence, as women writers since Hays and Wollstonecraft had been persistently pointing out, is a word loaded with economic meaning. For women, to have 'an independence' is to have your own money.

George Eliot's interest is in relationships. 'Independence' did not stir her artistically. Interdependence may have been her ideal, but the imbalances of feeling, the dependences and the repudiations between people, are the matter of her art. In particular, she is drawn to the representation of relationships where men and women are most dependent on each other. From *Romola* onwards, marriage and its difficulties became an absorbing theme.

*Romola* is the pivotal work in her growth as a woman writing. It is her least read and least appreciated work, and will probably always remain so. It is heavy going, replete with learning and with historical detail. All that is most powerful in it is most painful. The calm of the unflinching analysis is taxing in the extreme. Our rewards as readers are deeply wounding. The analysis of

Tito's moral decline and of the marriage between him and Romola grips and disturbs. It is this mixture of cumbersome detail and of excoriating insight which makes *Romola* hard to cope with for any willing reader. Our attention wakens us to trouble: and that is also what made the imagining of the work so energising for George Eliot.

The historical distance of the setting made it possible for her to explore more radical disturbances than she had ever confronted in her novels of English provincial life. The work imaged the possibility of profound upheaval in society. It represented extremes in emotional experience and behaviour which could not have been encompassed within the social realism of her earlier work. In order to give expression to extremity at the end of *The Mill* she was obliged to challenge the confines of social acceptance by moving outside the mode of realism she had adopted in the book. The river literally breaks its banks. The channel is swamped. Passion becomes obliterative. In *Romola*, because of the change in period, class, intellectual range of the characters, aesthetic preoccupations of the society, and the scholarly burden both of the characters' lives and of her own commensurate reading, she is able to engage formidable shifts in sensibility without having to abandon one kind of discourse for another. There is no exaggeration. There is great weight. Explaining her enterprise she commented on the need to create the medium of experience within the work:

> It is the habit of my imagination to strive after as full a vision of the medium in which a character moves as of the character itself. The psychological causes which prompted me to give such details of Florentine life and history as I have given, are precisely the same as those which determined me

114

in giving the details of English village life in *Silas Marner*, or the 'Dodson' life, out of which were developed the destinies of poor Tom and Maggie. (Carroll, 1971, p.206)

Yet, as the reviewer in the *Westminster Review* observed, there was the impress of the modern in the midst of Renaissance life.

> The conception of the marriage tie which underlies the whole story seems to us antedated by the whole interval which separates the age of Alexander VI from our own. We think it would be very difficult to produce any evidence of claims to the kind of union to which Romola aspired as existing in the minds of the women of the fifteenth century . . . . We cannot escape from the feeling that the chief interest of *Romola* reposes on ideas of moral duty and of right which are of very modern growth, and that they would have been more appropriately displayed on a modern stage. (Ibid., pp.216–17)

But could they have been so? As it was, critics were uneasy with the image of Tito and quickly feminised him: 'He is Hetty, but a man, and not a fool' (Ibid., p.217). Or Leslie Stephen dismisses Grandcourt and Tito together: 'Like Tito, he suggests to me at least, rather the cruel woman than the male autocrat' (Stephen, 1902, p.186). Stephen writes loftily, in a sentence whose significance turns back upon him: 'One feels, I think, that Grandcourt was drawn by a woman' (Stephen, 1902, p.186). One may 'feel' that, but for reasons other than his: reasons that have to do with the acumen with which she observes, unimplicated, Grandcourt's particularly eerie masculinity.

The reaction of Victorian critics to *Adam Bede* and *The Mill on the Floss*, despite their admiration for the works, suggests the limitations on subject-matter, the delicacies, which made it more possible for George Eliot to offer her critique of a marriage with the characters in the garb of 400 years ago.

> The lengthened treatment of a mystery so full of doubt and danger, by an Englishwoman writing for readers of both sexes, speaks as poorly for her good taste as the readiness wherewith a large-hearted girl yields up all her noble scruples, her tenderest sympathies, to the paltry fear of seeming cruel in the eyes of a weak, unworthy tempter, speaks, in our opinion, for her knowledge of human character. (Carroll, 1971, p.150)

George Eliot was no longer herself disguised by her man's name, so she re-clothed her characters. This replacement, as we have seen, was a permitting condition in her art. It was there as much in the abundance of metaphor as in the use of historical periods never quite her own—and it was there in her fascination with foster-parenting too. The author is now present as female in the text. 'George Eliot' becomes recognised as a female sign. This gave her some new freedoms. Swinburne may well be right, for instance, that representing Maggie as 'the willing or yielding companion of Stephen's flight would probably and deservedly have been resented as a brutal and vulgar outrage on the part of a male novelist' (Ibid., p.165). Though he is quite wrong in assuming that it is, therefore, an outrage on George Eliot's part, or some kind of underhand trick on her part as a woman writer.

Metaphor adopts the unkinned as kin. In that sense it is similar in its action to foster-relationships: developed affinities, and not descent, are the criterion for both. Approximation, not identity, becomes significant. As I have already argued, George Eliot is concerned with two concepts of kinship, kinship as descent within a patriarchal order in which property and authority move through the male line, and kinship as lateral connection: a newer concept of kin which had recently been immensely reinforced by Darwin's insistence on the 'infinite web' of connections between all living forms (Beer, 1983, pp. 149–80). Metaphor is preoccupied with likeness in the unlike. It eschews origins. It marks out connection, not descent. And in George Eliot's later books we can track a more and more determined move away from the accepted ideology of origins. So the inter-calating of past and present-day problems in *Romola* is no mere failure. Marriage is the closest and most sustained point of contact between self and other that her society had prepared. Man and wife are not original kin; they are not linked by descent though perhaps by affinity and certainly by circumstances.

   *Romola* accepts that vast changes have occurred in human experience since the Renaissance period it studies. Yet George Eliot applied to the analysis of that period, movements which established themselves in the nineteenth century, such as positivism and pre-Raphael-itism. This was not simple anachronism. It was an attempt to measure variation and continuity by means of 'analogical creation' (Pinney, 1963, p.446). In her late notes on 'historic imagination' she writes:

> By veracious imagination, I mean the working-out in detail of the various steps by which a political or social change was reached, using all extant evidence and supplying deficiencies by careful analogical creation. How triumphant opinions originally spread—how institutions arose—what were the conditions of great inventions, discoveries, or theoretic conceptions—what circumstances affecting individual lots are attendant on the decay of long-established systems,—all these grand elements of history require the illumination of special imaginative treatment. But effective truth in this

application of art requires freedom from the vulgar coercion of conventional plot. (p.446)

One thing that particularly fascinates her is the Whiggish tendency to write off movements that did not succeed as if they were less real than those that conquered. Equally 'A false kind of idealisation dulls our perception of the meaning in words when they relate to past events which have had a glorious issue' (Ibid., p.447). So we end up 'condemning in the present what we belaud in the past, and pronouncing impossible processes that have been repeated again and again in the historical preparation of the very system under which we live' (ibid.).

These words presage the concerns of *Daniel Deronda* more than they look back on the enterprise of *Romola*, but they help, I think, to explain the particular meaning that martyrdom and failure had for George Eliot. These, quite as much as triumph and fruitfulness, are part of the material of human experience and human society; they may give us a closer and more subtle access to the forces at work in cultures and in persons. The failure of the marriage between Romola and Tito is tracked with veracious imagination. As Carol Christ well shows in her article on 'Aggression and Providential Death in George Eliot's Fiction', George Eliot found scenes of confrontation disturbing to write. Christ sees the deflecting of confrontation as constraining the tragic scale of George Eliot's achievement. But in *Romola* the tragedy that George Eliot analyses with peculiar power is just the failure to confront, which is a strong temptation in marriage and which for Tito characterises his particular susceptibility to evil. The scene between Tito and Romola on the evening that he first wears the chain shirt to protect himself against assassination subtly registers how hard confrontation can be. Since this novel is less known, and its arcs of analysis are so long, I offer here some extended quotations.

> Tito, instead of meeting Romola's glance, closed his eyes and rubbed his hands over his face and hair. He felt he was behaving unlike himself, but he would make amends to-morrow. The terrible resurrection of secret fears, which, if Romola had known them, would have alienated her from him for ever, caused him to feel an alienation already begun between them—caused him to feel a certain repulsion towards a woman from whose mind he was in danger . . . .
> 'Ah, you have had so much to tire you to-day,' said Romola, kneeling down close to him, and laying her arm on his chest while she put his hair back caressingly.
> Suddenly she draw her arm away with a start, and a gaze of alarmed inquiry.
> 'What have you got under your tunic, Tito? Something as hard as iron.'
> 'It *is* iron—it is chain-armour,' he said at once. He was prepared for the surprise and the question, and he spoke quietly, as of something that he was not hurried to explain. (*Romola*, I, p.381, ch.27)

> 'But, dearest Tito,' she added, after a moment's pause, in a tone of loving anxiety, 'it will make you very wretched.'
> 'What will make me wretched?' he said, with a scarcely perceptible movement across his face, as from some darting sensation.
> 'This fear—this heavy armour. I can't help shuddering as I feel it under my arm. I could fancy it a story of enchantment—that some malignant fiend had changed your sensitive human skin into a hard shell. It seems so unlike my bright, light-hearted Tito!'
> 'Then you would rather have your husband exposed to danger, when he leaves you?' said Tito, smiling. 'If you don't mind my being poniarded or shot, why need I mind? I will give up the armour—shall I?'
> 'No, Tito, no. I am fanciful. Do not heed what I have said.' (*Romola*, I, p.383, ch.27)

Tito and Romola each retreat, tack and resist. The awkward fit of speech and description opens gaps and smudges barriers, 'caressingly', 'smiling'.

The moment of confrontation comes, however. The analysis of Romola's thought is supported and reinforced by analysis and metaphor. That of Tito is direct speech, unsustained by independent commentary:

> As that fluent talk fell on her ears there was a rising contempt within her, which only made her more conscious of her bruised, despairing love, her love for the Tito she had married and believed in. Her nature, possessed with the energies of strong emotion, recoiled from this hopelessly shallow readiness which professed to appropriate the widest sympathies and had no pulse for the nearest. She still spoke like one who was restrained from showing all she felt. She had only drawn away her arm from his knee, and sat with her hands clasped before her, cold and motionless as locked waters. (*Romola*, I, p.436, ch.32)

(The waters will flow again only after Tito's death when Romola drifts downstream, unconstrained.)

> 'I am sorry to hear you speak in that spirit of blind persistence, my Romola,' he said, quietly, 'because it obliges me to give you pain. But I partly foresaw your opposition, and as a prompt decision was necessary, I avoided that obstacle, and decided without consulting you. The very care of a husband for his wife's interests compels him to that separate action sometimes—even when he has such a wife as you, my Romola.' . . .
> 'You have *sold* them?' she asked, as if she distrusted her ears. 'I have,' said Tito, quailing a little. The scene was unpleasant—the descending scorn already scorched him. 'You are a treacherous man!' she said, with something grating in her voice, as she looked down at him. (I, p.438, ch.32)

The occasion and the excuse are both revealing. Tito has sold the library of Romola's dead father for dispersal, and to justify his action he uses the still-current argument of the husband's responsibility to act.

This book is full of the fragmenting and betraying of fathers. It is hard work to make them die, as Tito doubly discovers in his breaking-up of the library and in his repudiation of his foster-father Baldassare, whom he could have saved at great expense to himself, but whom he repudiates at the eventual cost of his life. Bardo, Romola's scholar-humanist father, has also been abandoned by his son, who has devoted his life to religious extremism. Tito has devoted his life to gentle hedonism, abandoning his scholar-father to slavery and death. Savonarola takes on the role of authoritarian father to all Florence (and because of his priestly status is always addressed as Father). He is eventually burned alive. Baldassare's superb memory—his whole range of learning—is restored to him only long enough to enable him to take vengeance on Tito and to die himself.

The extraordinary violence with which these images of the father are treated (and, in Baldassare, revenge themselves) suggests a psychodrama which has to do with the author's own need. But this need is able powerfully to express itself because it also represents 'pregnant movements' in human history (Pinney, 1963, p.447), removed from her own circumstances. She chooses the just pre-Raphaelite moment of a religious revulsion against humanism. (Raphael appears in the book as a boy of nine.)

In *Romola* George Eliot both shows how difficult is confrontation between intimates and for the first time relishes confrontation to the full: this empowers her imaginatively. She can include scenes of declamation such as Savonarola's preaching. She makes the past die

by means of the death of fathers and the death of their
learning. She acknowledges the end-stopping of history
in the death of individuals whether famous or obscure.
Yet she also urges the nemesis of the past, its vengeful
tendency to lie in wait. She writes, 'In strictness there is
no replacing of relations.' Only in the last part of the
book (which was the section that initiated her imagining
of it) does she suggest another possibility.

In a dream-like coda she represents Romola saving a
plague-stricken village of Jews. As in *The Mill on the Floss*,
new action is identified with drifting down water, but
where in *The Mill* Philip had dreamt of Maggie 'slipping
down a glistening, green, slimy channel of a waterfall'
(II, p.251), in a sexually jealous dream which preludes
her floating away with Stephen, here the floating
downstream is, for the character, wholly restorative
(and, for the reader, almost wholly unsatisfactory).
Whereas elsewhere in the work George Eliot has given
us a 'vivid presentation of how results have been actually
brought about, especially in religious and social change'
(Pinney, 1963, p.447) here she presents a 'utopian
picture'.

Having earlier bowed to the authority of Savonarola
and returned to her unloving and vitiating marriage,
Romola is now permitted infinite authority. She is
perceived first as 'the Holy Mother with the Babe' as she
approaches the village with the Hebrew child on her
arm. In this legendary guise, she tells a boy: 'I came over
the sea. I am hungry and so is the child. Will you not give
us some milk?' We recognise the hagiographic structure
which Anna Jameson had so thoroughly studied in
*Legends of the Madonna* (1852): the beggar makes a request
and is then revealed as saint or virgin. Earlier, in the
legend of St Ogg, George Eliot had used the apparition
of a

woman with a child in her arm; and she was clad in rags, and had a worn and withered look, and she craved to be rowed across the river . . . And he ferried her across. And it came to pass, when she stepped ashore, that her rags were turned into robes of flowing white. (*The Mill*, I, p.180, ch.12)

She is, of course, the 'Blessed Virgin'.

'You will fear no longer, father,' said Romola, in a tone of encouraging authority; 'you will come down with me, and we will see who is living, and we will look for the dead to bury them. I have walked about for months where the pestilence was, and see, I am strong.' (*Romola*, II, p.409, ch.65)

This testamental simplicity, in which Romola walks unscathed through pestilence and can distinguish the living and the dead, is in strange contrast to the sophisticated difficulty of the book's earlier analysis. It is as though the only discourse which George Eliot can trust when she seeks to express the vision of woman coming to authority is that of the saint's legend. And that is the story pattern she brings fully to the test in *Middlemarch*.

Anna Jameson, one of the best-known workers in the women's movement, a member of the Langham Place group, and a trusted adviser and older friend to women like Barbara Bodichon, had brought back into currency in the 1840s the legends of the Catholic Church, which, she argued, should be seen as offering an alternative set of symbolic insights to those available in the classics and for the majority of women, a more available one since classical learning was available primarily within an education system which excluded women at the time. Although it would be quite false to suggest that George Eliot—or indeed Anna Jameson—was excluded from classical learning, Jameson's work and its emphasis on hagiography as an alternative source of symbol had deep significance for George Eliot. She turns to Jameson's work again in *Middlemarch*, (Beer, 1983, pp.176-9). In *Sacred and Legendary Act* (1848), and *Legends of the Madonna* (1852), George Eliot, who knew Jameson well, found material for her own creativity.

Stephen Booth, Eric Trudgill and others have pointed out the prevalence of the Virgin as an image for the Victorians, but usually in relation with its assumed opposite, the whore or fallen woman. But what did it mean to George Eliot? Why the Madonna? In *Romola*, 'madonna' is used frequently as a simple term of address, equivalent to 'Madam', and this allows George Eliot to ease the transition between the divine and the ordinary and to keep the whole upon the plane of human affairs. The earthly, and independent, Romola who has borne no children of her own, and who is therefore close to the celibate, can freely foster Tessa's children and Tito's child-like other wife, Tessa. Such willing nurturing is very different from the physical involvement of childbearing which might have been the expected outcome for Romola. The Madonna here miraculously, perhaps over-miraculously, resolves the nature–nurture problem.

Bonnie Zimmerman comments on the attraction that George Eliot, both as a writer and woman, had for other women: recognising in her 'a transitional role-model . . . the image of Mother rushed to their minds, the one example of female power available in a patriarchy'. But, as Zimmerman also remarks, they also recognised in her 'The shattering of sexual stereotypes' (1980, pp.88). She refused to oppose 'Madonna' and 'fallen woman', binding them up in amity or combining them in her own person. So far as her art goes, though, it is the too thorough comfort of *Romola's* conclusion which is its weakness. To give comfort in George Eliot's work is blessed; to be comfortable is suspect. Both reader and writer are here allowed too great a measure of comfort. The conclusion of *Romola* is her one conformity to that possible ending which she had resisted in Bremer and Jewsbury: the woman on her estate, exempted from passion and passed into wisdom.

*Romola* encompasses George Eliot's insight at its most mordantly perceptive and its most unresistingly idealistic. The secure and powerful religious woman is recognised as a nostalgic image, and tempered with ever more complicated irony in the language of *Middlemarch*. The continuity between the two works is important. So is her way of disturbing in the figures of Dorothea, Casaubon and Will Ladislaw the easier and earlier contrast of good woman and weak man. But although we end alienated, with relief, from Tito, the process of reading the book exacts fellow feeling with him. The blaze of recognition in which the analysis engages us cannot avoid enforced self-knowledge. Tito is not unlike us. We are not permitted to identify solely with Romola. George Eliot's favourite form 'we' becomes a crucial channel for acceptance: either 'I' or 'you' would be unbearable. Men and women are not polarised, despite the figures here of strong woman/ weak man. The woman reading is not allowed self-satisfaction.

## II

*Silas Marner*, the work which interrupted and delayed *Romola*, is George Eliot's story which proves that 'magic is transcendent nature'. The folk-tale mode of the opening, the ballad-like elements in the story of Godfrey Cass and his secret marriage to opium addict Molly, Silas's uncanny trances, the mythic substitution of child for gold in a healing inversion of the Midas myth (where Midas unwittingly turns his little daughter into a gold statue): all these elements declare the extent to which the work draws on fairy-tale to sustain its transformations.

The figure of Silas, bent and isolated, has overtones of Rumpelstiltskin, another male weaver with a penchant for babies. But these allusions (Midas, Rumpelstiltskin, the Norns), are all there to be lost and obliterated. They are part of the system of expectation and allusion which we must respond to, and dispel, if we are to reach the human directness of the work. The manifest is here, peculiarly, the meaning. Silas is not feminised; he is not a woman. He is a man, a celibate, who nurtures a girl-child and thus becomes her father. As she wrote, George Eliot seems to have determined to demonstrate how far transformation is a human power, and in the figure of Silas she sets out to show how not only his, but his society's assumptions, are changed.

Silas is a weaver, deliberately set *across* the stereotype of the woman weaving, which, though it may have derived from social practice in ancient Greece, certainly did not correspond to conditions after the onset of the industrial revolution in England. 'The Fates at their weaving' was a familiar literary trope, but home-weaving was already largely a thing of the past at the time George Eliot wrote and was no longer a woman's occupation.

*Silas Marner* humanises George Eliot's increasing fascination with the action of chance. This fascination was intellectually reinforced by Darwin's insistence on 'chance' mutation as happening to fit or unfit an organism for its medium, but it was also forced on her by her practice as a novelist. In an excellent analysis George Levine (1962) has analysed the functions of determinism in George Eliot's work; but we are equally made aware of coincidence, of the haphazard assemblage of circumstances by which things come to be. The process can be most acutely observed where there is a secret to be kept. As the narrative comments in *The Mill on the Floss*:

> Secrets are rarely betrayed or discovered according to any programme our fear has sketched out. Fear is almost always haunted by terrible dramatic scenes, which recur in spite of the best-argued probabilities against them .... Those slight indirect suggestions which are dependent on apparently trivial coincidences and incalculable states of mind, are the favourite machinery of Fact, but are not the stuff in which imagination is apt to work. (II, p.110, Bk.V, ch.5)

This commentary describes a technical problem for the novelist: the reader may more readily be reconciled to dream-scenes of discovery and confrontation than to the minute operations of the trivial and incalculable. We have already seen in 'The Lifted Veil' that George Eliot was as much aware of the factitiousness of concealing the contrivances in a narrative as of the disruptiveness of laying them open. The writer makes choices. Does that make her also responsible for the events of the work? Must she become the book's 'transcendental signifier', occupying the place of God the Father? Since, outside the fiction, George Eliot rejected the figure of God and was declaredly against any belief in personal providence and personal after-life, this technical problem was one she shared at the opposite end of the spectrum with Muriel Spark. Spark delights in manifesting chance, plot, contrivance, as a representation of divine plotting, a plot inscrutable and uncomfortable but unavoidably in charge. Ideologically, George Eliot needed to find a quite other organisation for plot. She needed one which would allow sufficient capaciousness for coincidence to issue from the largesse of possibility without any implication of plan. This was the method she took to its fullest extent in *Middlemarch*, but even there she found it necessary to turn to law as narrative metaphor. Law, and lawyers' confidentiality and strategy, could figure the ineluctable connections of unlike which manifest themselves as coincidence.

Coincidence functions in narrative in a way similar to that of rhyme in poetry or pun in sentence. The pleasure comes in part from a sense of the randomly contiguous proving to have shared meaning—or, rather, having joint meaning exacted from them. There is an element of the wilful in such achievement, a wilfulness which subtly reveals itself in the skill with which it is almost obliterated. The chanciness of rhyme, pun and coincidence bring to the fore the extent of the purely contingent. Yet, paradoxically, there is a trace of some underlying design imputed. Coincidence may privilege teleology: that is, it implies a providence which shapes our ends, rough hew them how we will. In that way, it dangerously reinforces the supremacy of the writer, even while it appears at the level of event to flout the concept of order.

George Eliot needs and uses coincidence. The unforeseen in her work, however, is rooted in individual history. She humanises coincidence rather than allowing it any transcendental level. Nemesis is the outcome of many choices. The generative acts of human beings go on for ever 'like sound waves'. Coincidence is in large measure a matter of paying attention. We are surrounded continuously by coincidences. We observe them only when they challenge, confirm, or play into our preoccupations. It is for that reason that the level of coincidence rises sharply when we fall in love. Writing fiction generates the same kind of total attentiveness as love. So at one level, we may argue that the taken-for-granted quality of coincidence in much of her earlier work has to do with the activity of creating: coincidence is revealed by the process of writing. But she less and less overseals coincidence; instead she makes it stand out. At the same time, she increasingly naturalises it as kin. Hidden parentage and shared descent force her figures to acknowledge kinships hitherto ignored.

George Eliot does not give much credit to the luxury of shattering. Shards, fragmented interruptions, and absences have, in her work, a way indefatigably of reconnecting themselves to hitherto unconsidered elements in the work's economy. The process can be quite as much menacing as reassuring. Knitting up is the activity of the fates as much as it is of old Dutch women in seventeenth-century art. It is the activity of gossips, writers and, at least in stereotype, women (even if we reject Freud's claim that women's only contribution to civilisation is spinning and weaving in a symbolic attempt to conceal their own debilitated genitals).

Gilbert and Gubar give a sentimentally benign analysis of the activity of 'yarning'—a benignity validated by Joycean puns with their assertion of power over language. But puns, like rhymes, register the subtle alliance of random elements which may as well oppress as liberate. Coincidence, as the narrative form of pun or rhyme, displays the helplessness of organised sequence. George Eliot excels at recording the hidden motions of connection. Congruence and confluence are movements that fascinate her artistically, and the predominance of providential deaths may come about because she cannot imagine any mode of alienation other than death absolute enough to free the individual from connection. Even death, moreover, works to liberate only spouses, not children. Her remark in the course of her review of Riehl that we are 'incarnate history' is peculiarly apt for women who bear children.

Kin is a more profound naturalisation of coincidence than law can ever be. Kin is the point of oscillation between nature and culture and for nineteenth century novelists, in particular, carried the burden of genetic and social determinations. But George Eliot, more than Balzac or Zola, brought out the oddity of being kin: the improbable welding of one to another, the dangerous fleeting resemblances and the deep unlikenesses. She made such awkward proximities the topic of *The Mill*, in which she also showed their profoundly binding effects. In *Silas Marner*, on the other hand, nurture predominates over nature, and chance over the predeterminations of ordered sequence. The book opens by showing us Silas Marner falsely found guilty through the drawing of lots (chance figures there either as divine intervention or random throws); it suspends Silas's consciousness by a cataleptic fit at what prove to be two crucial moments (the stealing of his gold and the arrival of the child Eppie) and it thereby makes a link between the two events which suggests that they are akin. The money has represented order to Silas in a world become enigma and has given a shape to his life which keeps death further off:

> In this strange world, made a hopeless riddle to him, he might, if he had had a less intense nature, have sat weaving, weaving—looking towards the end of his pattern, or towards the end of his web, till he forgot the riddle, and

everything else but his immediate sensations; but the money had come to mark off his weaving into periods, and the money not only grew, but it remained with him. (*Silas Marner*, p.27, ch.2)

The geometry of his design, like the obsessional activity of a man 'shut up in solitary confinement' marks 'the moments by straight strokes of a certain length on the wall, until the growth of the sum of straight strokes, arranged, in triangles, has become a mastering purpose' (ibid.). Eppie appears to Silas's blurred vision as hard gold but as soon as he touches her, he feels the softness of hair, a 'sleeping child—a round, fair thing, with soft yellow rings all over its head'. Geometry yields to growing life. Silas's touching of Eppie restores him to life and frees him from gold, in an inversion of the Midas story. That sentence is immediately followed by: 'Could this be his little sister come back to him in a dream—his little sister whom he had carried about in his arms for a year before she died, when he was a small boy with-shoes or stockings?' (*Silas Marner*, p.170, ch.12). The immediate mention of his childhood experience with his sister again removes the magical, or merely wish-fulfilling, in the story.

The view, assigned in *Adam Bede* to the misogynist Bartle Massey, that men as well as women are capable of parenting, is here given full meaning as it will be again in the relationship of Rufus Lyon and Esther in *Felix Holt*. In both cases, the fostering relationship removes the authoritarian pressure of descent. The celibate man parenting the girl-child is a strange re-reading of the mentor–pupil relationship which George Eliot views with increasing doubt and asperity as her career advances. Perhaps one can see in this relationship traces of what Dorothy Dinnerstein (1978, p.158) holds to typify a particular kind of creative sustenance. She takes as an example the relationship between George Eliot and George Lewes, in which the man takes on the nurturing role. Nancy Chodorow in *The Reproduction of Mothering* (1978) argues that anyone who has been well parented has the 'relational basis' for parenting and asks, 'What happens to potential parenting capacities in men?'

In this small but profound work George Eliot shows Silas, sustained by Dolly Winthrop's pungent advice, bringing up Eppie, and thereby becoming again part of the community of humankind. George Eliot reminds us by means of the epigraph to *Silas Marner* that the warmest and most loving upbringing cannot guarantee the future. Wordsworth's Michael, also, had parented Luke fully and lovingly. Her epigraph quotes the lines:

> 'A child, more than all other gifts
> That earth can offer to declining man,
> Brings hope with it, and forward-looking thoughts.'

Yet Luke fell into bad ways. The Wordsworthian references in the book grasp the knottiness of human life. But in this idyll such possibilities are raised simply to frame the happier outcome here.

The punishing hand, writing, prescribes the fate of Godfrey Cass, Eppie's natural father, whose 'motherly' wife, Nancy, loses her baby. When Godfrey comes to reclaim Eppie fifteen years later he is made to recognise the impotence of parental authority without nurturing love. The claims are set out in terms of class conflict: as in *Adam Bede*, the claims on the part of the governing classes to foster an organic community are shown to be a sham. Godfrey asserts:

> 'She may marry some low working-man, and then, whatever I might do for her, I couldn't make her well-off.

You're putting yourself in the way of her welfare; and though I'm sorry to hurt you after what you've done, and what I've left undone, I feel now that it's my duty to insist on taking care of my own daughter. I want to do my duty.'...
... 'I can't feel as I've got any father but one,' said Eppie, impetuously, while the tears gathered. 'I've always thought of a little home where he'd sit i' the corner, and I should fend and do everything for him: I can't think o' no other home. I wasn't brought up to be a lady, and I can't turn my mind to it. I like the working-folks, and their victuals, and their ways. And,' she ended passionately, while the tears fell, 'I'm promised to marry a working-man, as 'll live with father, and help me to take care of him.' (pp.256, 259, ch.19)

George Eliot questions in *Silas Marner* the organicist emphasis on descent as a justifying and sufficient metaphor.

# III

When she comes to write *Felix Holt* she looks at the contradictions within political radicalism, with its suggestion of uprooting and new beginnings, while assumptions about basic relationships—those between men and women—are yet to remain unquestioned. Her work on parenting and fostering in *Romola* and *Silas Marner*, and her fiercely intimate yet distanced enquiry into marriage in *Romola*, continue to fuel and trouble *Felix Holt the Radical*.

The energy of *Felix Holt the Radical* is in the friction between the pseudo-radicalism of politics and the entrenched conservatism of practice of Harold Transome and even of Felix himself. The most memorable figures in the book are those at the opposite poles of feeling: Mrs

Transome and Rufus Lyon. The book's narrative is rigorously yoked together by the complicated legal tangle which will reveal Esther Lyon as the lawful inheritor of the Transome estate. In a witty compression of roles, the lawyer, Jermyn, is also the secret father of Harold Transome. Transome is bent on ousting Jermyn from his position of trust in the management of the estate. One problem in the work is that the arch-conservative, Mrs Transome, is far and away the most radical person in feeling. Her life raises questions which challenge the orthodoxies of Victorian sexual mores to a far greater extent than Felix ever succeeds in challenging the political ideas and practice of the time. This may be because Mrs Transome is fired by the emotion that, artistically, George Eliot seems to have found most thrilling: remorse. The narrative half-recounts and hints at stories told by the coachman, Sampson, to his passengers. The stories make frivolous public currency out of what is yet still concealed and private in the minds of those they concern. 'Pub-talk' cannot be controlled: its formulaic ribaldry lays bare what is simultaneously elsewhere obsessionally secret.

> At least Sampson was right in saying that there had been fine stories—meaning, ironically, stories not altogether creditable to the parties concerned. And such stories often come to be fine in a sense that is not ironical. For there is seldom any wrong-doing which does not carry along with it some downfall of blindly-climbing hopes, some hard entail of suffering, some quickly-satiated desire that survives, with the life in death of old paralytic vice, to see itself cursed by its woeful progeny—some tragic mark of kinship in one brief life to the far-stretching life that went before, and to the life that is to come after, such as has raised the pity and terror of men ever since they began to discern between will and destiny. (*Felix Holt*, I, pp. 12–13, Introduction)

The re-emergence of the symbolic language of Greek drama becomes marked in George Eliot's later books: for example, Richard Jenkyn has analysed the meaning of the *Medea* in the allusions of *Felix Holt*; and the terrible figures of the Furies begin to stalk through the writing, emerging as whisper and echo in *Daniel Deronda*. The force of Mrs Transome's fears, cramped within immoveable past events, projected as compelling future images, gives *Felix Holt* much of its power. Her absence throughout the middle section of the novel brings an accompanying drop in the book's capacity for innovation.

Most critics have commented on the very unradical nature of Felix's radicalism: 'The Radicalism of *Felix Holt* is strangely remote from the reader . . . We find him a Radical and we leave him what?—only 'utterly married'; which is all very well in its place, but which by itself makes no conclusion', writes Henry James. (Carroll, 1971, p.275). Is the marriage a recession from Radicalism? Are politics and sexual politics disjoined, or are they too easily elided in this work? Arnold Kettle, though not making any link between proletarian and feminist politics, strongly argues that we should respect the substance of Holt's arguments although 'he is not allowed to grapple in a serious way with the actual problems of popular leadership, and his very inadequacies in this respect are paraded as virtues' (Hardy, 1970, p.110).

Linda Bamber (1975, p.434) suggests that George Eliot's 'sense of sexual politics . . . cannot be sustained or used structurally'. Bonnie Zimmerman disagrees: '*Felix Holt*, by counterpointing woman's role with radical politics, makes the structures perfectly clear' (1979, p.433). Gilbert and Gubar allude only to the women, never concerning themselves with possible connections between active class politics and feminism. E.S. Dallas, always one of George Eliot's most perceptive commentators, remarked that the work is 'not . . . a political novel, though it necessarily touches on politics . . . . The hero of the tale, therefore, is rather a moral and a social than a political reformer' (Carroll, 1971, pp.265–6). John Morley saw the puzzle of the book as 'the evil usage which women receive at the hands of men' (Carroll, 1971, p.255). So far as I have discovered, none of her contemporaneous critics made a connection between these two aspects of the novel, as we would do now. Indeed, this is one of the instances where one can readily radicalise George Eliot way beyond her own control. By this I mean that this book potentiates radical questioning without itself being in command of it.

Bamber is right to point out that George Eliot makes no attempt to bridge the private domain inhabited by the women, and the public inhabited by the men. But the book *opens* with the suppression of a woman's independence, a suppression which has been previously put at her works' conclusion, and therefore out of reach of question. Mrs Transome has been running her estate without any help from her feeble-minded husband for a number of years, aided only by the legal acumen (and self-seeking embezzling, Harold later suggests) of Jermyn, long ago her lover and now a distant colleague.

In approaching the connections between women and politics in this novel, it is worth recalling that Comte saw his work as depending particularly on 'the support of women and the proletary class'. In the preface of the *Catechism of Positive Religion* (translated by Richard Congreve, whose wife was a particular friend of George Eliot, in 1858) Comte says that the 'positive philosophy' addresses itself particularly to women:

Woman's object is everywhere the same, to secure the due supremacy of moral force; so she is led to visit with especial reprobation all collective violence. (Comte, 1858, p.36)

The catechism is arranged as a colloquy between woman and priest, a colloquy in which the woman poses the problems and the priest provides explanations. In structure, and in some of its opinions, the Comte *Catechism* seems quite as inclined simultaneously to idealise and imprison women as are many religious systems. But, as G.H. Lewes remarked, George Eliot had taught him to read Comte's religion of humanity as utopian expression rather than as a programme of reform and it provides a tonic analysis of many then-current social assumptions.

One striking distinction that Comte draws out may have had particular force in George Eliot's developing argument with herself and within her works about the signification of motherhood:

*The Woman*—The instincts, as a whole, seem placed in their right light, except the maternal instinct. This I expected to find under the head of altruism, not under that of egoism.

*The Priest*—You must distinguish, my daughter, between the maternal instinct and the influence that instinct may have on our sympathies . . . However valuable the improvement effected by civilization, particularly modern civilization, in this instinct, as a consequence of the increasing influence of society on the family, it is yet possible, in daily experience, to detect its true nature in women of weak sympathies, where it stands out more distinctly. In such cases we see that the child, for the mother no less than for the father, is regarded directly in the light of a mere personal possession, on which they may exercise their love of power, or by which they may gratify their avarice, far more than as the object of any disinterested affection. (Ibid., p.261)

In *Felix Holt* George Eliot establishes a similar distinction between the expansion of power and of feeling in motherhood.

> The mother's love is at first an absorbing delight, blunting all other sensibilities; it is an expansion of the animal existence; it enlarges the imagined range for self to move in: but in after years it can only continue to be joy on the same terms as other long-lived love—that is, by much suppression of self, and power of living in the presence of another. (Felix Holt, I, p.32, ch.1)

The emphasis on the moral power of woman and of the proletariat could have made a link other than an active political one in her mind between two classes. (Comte wanted both classes privatised and centred on the family, while yet somehow suffusing their influence through general social orders.)

The return of her son puts an end to Mrs Transome's command and independence. Her revolt always takes the form of defeat. She is without hope, oppressed by dread, incapable of acting because never able to make herself heard, and yet speaking trenchant truths which go unnoticed.

Sadoff comments that 'The authority of narration belongs to male narrators because Eliot envisions the traditions of storytelling as *patriarchal and genealogical*' (Sadoff, 1982, p.109; emphasis added). She is referring here particularly to the coachman, Mr Sampson's introduction of *Felix Holt*. But one of the ironies of the book is that if *law is male story* ('patriarchal and genealogical'), as its identification with Jermyn and its patriarchal organisation of inheritance imply, that story unexpectedly produces a female inheritor—Esther Lyon —and one at liberty to repudiate her inheritance. Mrs Transome strongly identifies herself with Esther, in an unforeseen way, and looks on her as the daughter she might have had.

During the 1860s, from the evidence of her notebooks and her later novels, George Eliot became increasingly concerned with anthropological explanations for the exclusion of women from family inheritance and from property rights. Gone is that facetious tone of her early 1850s comment that women do not deserve much better than men allow them. Instead she cites explanations of family and social organisation, such as Bachofen's *Das Mutterrecht*.

> Bachofen (*das Mutterrecht*) thinks that communal marriage was the primitive condition, but that after a while the women, shocked & scandalized at such a state of things, revolted against & established a system of marriage with female supremacy, the husband being subject to the wife, & women enjoying the principal share of political power. The first period he calls that of Hetairism, the second of *Mutterrecht*.
> The origin of Civilization & primitive Condition of Man. Lubbock. (Pratt, 1979, pp.445)

She follows this passage satirically with Bachofen's comment that in breaking away from female supremacy man raised his gaze to the higher regions of the cosmos; and for good measure adds a biting anecdote:

> Bachofen, again, explains the change from male to female relationship thus: 'Man durchbricht die Bänden des Tellurismus und erhebt seinen Blick zu den höhern Regionen des Cosmos'!
> 'What,' said a negro to Burton, 'am I to starve [crossed out: that] while my sister has children whom she can sell?' (Ibid.)

Summarising Henry Maine's, *Ancient Law: its Connection*

*with the Early History of Society and its Relation to Modern Ideas*
(London, 1861) George Eliot, in 1869, noted the
comments: 'Mulier est finis familiae' (Ibid., p.204); and
'None of the descendants of a female . . . are included in
the primitive notion of a family relationship.' (Ibid.,
p.262) No wonder that George Eliot remarked caustically in the margin, 'The modern position of women is
chiefly determined by barbarian elements.'

George Eliot read Maine after writing *Felix Holt*, but, as
we saw in the Chapman article quoted earlier, which was
published alongside Marian Evans' in the mid-1850s,
there was already in the 1850s and 1860s an increasing
awareness of the exclusion of women by means of law
within many cultures. We find this depicted more fully
in *Middlemarch* where, Pratt and Neufeldt remark, the
truth of George Eliot's comments on Maine are
'demonstrated . . . by the plight of Aunt Julia and the
debarment of Ladislaw, related to Casaubon on the
female side, from the family fortune' (Ibid., p.262). So
the legal ramifications of the middle section of *Felix Holt*
are not as distant from sexual politics as may at first
appear. The patriarchal succession of genealogy, combined with the fiction of the law, here, in a somewhat
wishful twist to the story, unexpectedly put a woman in
control and bring about the father's downfall. Jermyn,
maker of story through legal manipulation, and adulter-
er of others' story-line (who begat Harold Transome?)
bears the negative responsibility for narrative. His
activity exempts from intervention that 'George Eliot'
inscribed on the title page.

Esther can choose her inheritance and her class. Like
Eppie before her, she can move to the upper classes or
remain with her adoptive father and her lover. Whereas
in *Silas Marner* the whole emphasis was on the
relationship between father and daughter, here the

stress of a much more developed analysis is on the relationship between Esther and Felix. The common Victorian reward for the fictional heroine (as in Disraeli's *Sybil*) is to discover yourself a scion of an aristocratic family and to move up socially to claim your birthright. The reward of working-class enterprise, in novels such as *Salem Chapel*, is to move into the bourgeoisie. Neither Esther nor Felix make the accustomed fictional move. Esther identifies with her foster-father—indeed, she moves towards him with more affection when she discovers that he *is* her foster-father and not her natural father. She begins more thoroughly to respect him. The commentary describes the history of Esther's life within the book as a 'revolutionary struggle'. This seems an exaggeration.

> But life is measured by the rapidity of change, the succession of influences that modify the being; and Esther had undergone something little short of an inward revolution. The revolutionary struggle, however, was not quite at an end. (*Felix Holt*, I, p.340, ch.49)

Esther's inward revolution is completed in her night meeting with Mrs Transome, when at last Harold has discovered his paternity and Mrs Transome is utterly isolated.

> They turned hand in hand into the room, and sat down together on a sofa at the foot of the bed. The disordered gray hair—the haggard face—the reddened eyelids under which the tears seemed to be coming again with pain, pierced Esther to the heart. A passionate desire to soothe this suffering woman came over her. She clung round her again, and kissed her poor quivery lips and eyelids, and laid her young cheek against the pale and haggard one. Words could not be quick or strong enough to utter her yearning....

'I have been an unhappy woman, dear.'

'I feared it,' said Esther, pressing her gently.

'Men are selfish. They are selfish and cruel. What they care for is their own pleasure and their own pride.'

'Not all,' said Esther, on whom these words fell with a painful jar.

'All I have ever loved,' said Mrs Transome. (II, pp.347–8, ch.50)

The scene of deep intimacy between the old and the young woman relates to an apothegm presented a little earlier:

> When a woman feels purely and nobly, that ardour of hers which breaks through formulas too rigorously urged on men by daily practical needs, makes one of her most precious influences: she is the added impulse that shatters the stiffening crust of cautious experience (II, p.313, ch.46)

George Eliot cut out that sentence in the Cabinet edition. Why? Perhaps she found the tone of the latter part too insistent; or was it because she had come to see it as too complicit with contemporary views of 'woman's mission'?

Esther and Felix are the survivors of the book, but Mrs Transome in her bitterness is its progenitor. Like the Princess Halm-Eberstein in *Daniel Deronda*, her words move us in directions different from her fate. Both women are punished, yet both have a powerful testamental force which can never be written out of the novel. Moreover, Mrs Transome provokes in the narrative discourse a wry obduracy of tone more absolute than we meet elsewhere in George Eliot's work: 'It is a fact perhaps kept a little too much in the background, that mothers have a self larger than their maternity.' Zimmerman (p.444) suggests that George

Eliot's resentment and anger at the price she had paid herself for sexual 'misconduct' take a new form in the identification with Mrs Transome: 'This may also be why so little irony and direct moral commentary undermine the integrity of her passion and anger, or why no other character is allowed to have the final word.' In the work's insistence on the private domain of women and its enforced separation from the public domain George Eliot intensifies the private/public split so that it is shown as the matter of tragedy, not of good order.

One of her most famous statements concerning the interconnection of the private and public occurs at the start of the book; but in the light of what happens in *Felix · Holt* it is worth the reader looking again at that passage, and noting that the milkmaid who must follow the tribe is an active part of the community with a task within it. The horror of Mrs Transome's position is her power-lessness, and her lack (once Harold has usurped her) of proper occupation. Suffering may be so private that it is never committed to writing: 'committed to no sound except that of low moans in the night, seen in no writing except that made on the face by the slow months of suppressed anguish and early morning tears' (I, p.13, Introduction). Mrs Transome's brooding vehemence can express itself only as petty power—a fiction of power with which to ease her powerlessness.

> Her part in life had been that of the clever sinner, and she was equipped with the views, the reasons, and the habits which belonged to that character: life would have little meaning for her if she were to be gently thrust aside as a harmless elderly woman. (pp.22–3)

Although George Eliot, brooding on the mother's love,

at first sounds like Comte, the commentary later sounds more like Chodorow (1978, pp.86–8).

Mrs Transome has looked for *recognition* from Harold — a recognition of her independent being as the ground of a renewal of love. Reciprocity has been her hope; scant stereotypes are what she receives. The venom with which she acknowledges her powerlessness is the only remaining form of power, and even that is silenced in Harold's presence. The growth of the child of adultery to full manhood and physical likeness to his unsuspected father is the form her dread takes (twice in early chapters we hear about their similar plump white hands, but like a skilful suspense writer George Eliot embroils the detail sufficiently for us not to become aware of it). Harold is, instructively, worsted by the same stereotypes that curtail his relations to his mother. His first wife, from Muscat, is sketched in by innuendo as a voluptuous domestic slave. His views of Esther are limited by the same assumptions.

> There was a lightning that shot out of her now and then, which seemed the sign of a dangerous judgement; as if she inwardly saw something more admirable than Harold Transome. Now, to be perfectly charming, a woman should not see this. (II, p.252, ch.43)

One of the more remarkable effects of the novel is to make the Oedipus story comparatively unimportant in comparison with that of Medea. When Jermyn and Harold have their murderous encounter and Harold discovers his paternity, we feel satisfaction. But the absolute truncating of his relationship with his mother —the *absence* of any erotic awareness—shows him stultified by his own lack of parentage. At one point, George Eliot appropriates the tale of the parts of the body and the stomach from *Coriolanus*. Harold, like Coriolanus, wishes to live 'as if a man were author of himself/ And knew no other kin.' But unlike Coriolanus, who bows to the pleas of his mother and his wife, Harold remains locked within the meagre concept of manhood which he has adopted, mitigated only a little by his concessive visit to his mother at the end. Felix, on the other hand, though often unsatisfactorily characterised in his declarative hectoring mode, is shown to be capable of recognition and change, a capacity shown also in his power to awaken change.

The private world of the woman extends outwards to test the men in the book. Perhaps this shows a political idealism which presents women's behaviour and women's realm as a better model for story than the legalistic fable of succession entailed upon the male line and male values. It would be pleasing to believe that, but I cannot do so. Instead, the connection between the *uselessness* of Mrs Transome's growing rage and the deafness of all political parties to what is meant by change, remains the radical insight of the book. We are led to participate in two unuseable possibilities, both of which are discounted and mocked by the everyday world: Rufus Lyon's community Christianity with its cloudy discourse and its absolute values, and Mrs Transome's vengeful imprecations against a world organised to exclude her voice while paying her all-enclosing respects.

In a narrative form so preoccupied with issues of cause and effect, George Eliot brought increasingly into question the reliance on 'natural law' as a determining explanation of interpenetrating forces. Natural law, with its presumption of fixed sequence and of irremoveable biological factors, could easily become a means of oppressing women, curtailing the space in which it was possible for them to act. Some of Marian Lewes's utterances outside the novels seem to show that she shared the emphasis of her age on women's physical nature as circumscribing their possibilities, but the works of fiction offer a more intense and yet more hesitant yoking and conjoining of diverse stories. She wrote in a letter towards the end of her career that the meaning of her books lay more in their structures than in their statements. If we take this seriously, we may learn something about the peculiar dilemma she discovered. The imbalances and awkwardness of fit between stories that she yet showed to be deeply interconnected, in *Felix Holt* and *Daniel Deronda* particularly, demonstrate the problem she had in sustaining any confidence in the reality of single-direction movement. Yet narrative labours if it is entirely lateral, a knot of interconnections. She could not easily imagine revolution. (Though at the end of *Daniel Deronda* in a geographically displaced and idealised way she tried.) At the same time, conclusions figure themselves always as a willed geometry in her fictional structures (for example, the finale of *Middlemarch* and the Milton quotation at the end of *Daniel Deronda*).

Increasingly, too, she repudiated that dependence on explicable origins which gives much of the passion to the study of causality. Instead she demonstrates how the stories we habitually cast as conclusive, always give access to new beginnings; the Genesis myth is one of the most important forms of this perception. She alludes to that myth in the Finale to *Middlemarch*. So for her, the idea of descent and kin begins to be realised in contradictory imaginative modes: as a binding system which makes the meaning of the present dependent on the past; or, as a precipitous rush into a future beyond the control of will or of parenthood.

Chapter Six

# *Middlemarch* and 'The Woman Question'

'Since I can do no good because a woman,
Reach constantly at something that is near it'.
Beaumont and Fletcher, *The Maid's Tragedy*
(Epigraph to *Middlemarch*, Chapter I)

## *I*

The first reviewers of *Middlemarch* were in little doubt about the book's intended topic: it was the nature and the education of women, and the question of society's responsibility for women's difficulties. R.H. Hutton, reviewing Book II (the novel appeared in parts) commented that

the thesis of the 'Prelude' that 'these blundering lives are due to the inconvenient indefiniteness with which the Supreme Power has fashioned the nature of women' ... requires the obtrusion of the notion of mistake and chance throughout the tale. (Carroll, 1971, p.291)

147

Reviewing the whole work, he complains that George Eliot overemphasises 'a bad public opinion about women' as responsible for Dorothea's marriages. He claims that 'little or no attempt is made to trace the connection in this book'; George Eliot's attempt, he writes, 'to represent the book as an elaborate contribution to the "Woman's" question seems to us a mistake' (Ibid., p.307). He then offers an astute analysis of the Lydgate/ Rosamond marriage and of 'the perverted public opinion' which leads to mistaken valuation of 'that mere semblance of tenderness which is called feminine grace'. He has taken in the book's intimation that Lydgate was 'misled through sharing the blundering notion of an age in which men and women have few intellectual interests in common'. But he evades his own perception that such issues were related to current controversy within the women's movement by claiming that 'the type of woman represented by Rosamond is far too unique to be much of a contribution towards the "woman" question' (ibid., p.308).

*Middlemarch* is about more than women and the women's movement, but those concerns are crucial to the questions raised within the work and are intimately connected with its narrative procedures. What is remarkable is the extent to which the feminist issues of the work were recognised as crucial, and quite specific, by the book's first readers but then, in critics of the next 100 years until the 1970s, were hardly discussed at all. A vital level of the text became invisible, it seems. Virginia Woolf is an honourable and obvious exception, but elsewhere the context of controversy on which the book draws simply went underground. It is tonic to recognise how fully this work was in touch with the issues being debated in the women's movement of the 1850s and 1860s, and how thoroughly it entered the debates.

The anonymous reviewer in the *Saturday Review* is alarmed lest 'our young ladies' may 'take to be Dorotheas' and 'to regulate their own conduct on the system of a general disapproval of the state of things into which they are born' (ibid., p.315). Dorothea, to this critic, is subversive in her 'strength of opinions', and her tendency to act upon them. He contrasts her unfavourably with Celia, who 'not feeling it her duty to subvert the world . . . can take her place in it naturally' (Ibid., p.316) ('Naturally' is always an indicative word in such argument.)

> But surely it is not every girl's duty to refuse the advantages and pleasures of the condition in which she finds herself because all do not share them. She is not selfish because she is serenely happy in a happy home. (Ibid.)

The alarm this critic feels concerns the connecting of the 'woman question' with questions of economics and class. The inequities of society are condensed in Dorothea's ill-formulated but earnest wishes to reform the social order—wishes whose activity is limited by her own oppression as a woman. 'Women were expected to have weak opinions' (I, p.4, ch.1). Dorothea does not for a long time understand her own predicament, but as readers we are made to perceive it from the outset, as this critic unwillingly has done.

The Shirreff sisters commented on the dislike of 'decision' in women in *Thoughts on Self Culture: Addressed to Women* (London 1850):

> The general system of female education, . . . so far from cultivating decision of character as an essential feature of moral strength, carefully represses even the natural tendency to it, treating it as a sign of presumption, or of *obstinacy*. Girls are reproved instead of encouraged, when

they attempt to exercise their judgement, and to act on their own principles, and in this manner not only are their reasoning powers weakened by the habit of adopting conclusions of the most important nature without investigation, but their moral vigour is impaired, owing to the action of inferior motives only on the will. (Shirreff, 1854 Edn, p.204)

Dorothea's marriage becomes a 'nightmare of life in which every energy was arrested by dread' and only with others is she able to have 'the relief of pouring forth her feelings unchecked'. She possesses 'a full current of sympathetic motive in which her ideas and impulses were habitually swept along'. When she comes to encourage Mr Brooke to improve the management of his estate alongside his attempt to enter Parliament as 'a member who cares for the improvement of the people' she speaks in a 'clear and unhesitating' voice, urging him to think of Kit Downes,

> 'who lives with his wife and seven children in a house with one sitting-room and one bedroom hardly larger than this table! . . . . I think we have no right to come forward and urge wider changes for good, until we have tried to alter the evils which lie under our own hands.' (II, pp.175–6, ch.39)

Sarah Ellis, discussing the 'conversation of the women of England', would certainly have seen this outburst as 'tasteless':

> the *habit* of acting from that first and most powerful impulse of our nature, and just pouring forth the fullness of our own hearts, discharging our own imagination of its load . . . without regard to fitness or preparation in the soil upon which the seed may fall . . . renders conversation sometimes tasteless . . . and sometimes inexpressibly annoying. (Ellis, 1838, p.137)

George Eliot's chosen metaphors ('impulse', 'pouring', 'discharging') are polemically opposed to earlier valuations, such as Mrs Ellis's, of those words in relation to women. By their means George Eliot expresses generosity of mind and of sexuality, both 'sometimes inexpressibly annoying' to society. Even Will Ladislaw, feeling that at that moment Dorothea is 'unmindful of him', experiences 'a chilling sense of remoteness'. The commentary caustically brings into question the idea of 'nature' and natural attributes: 'A man is seldom ashamed of feeling that he cannot love a woman so well when he sees a certain greatness in her: nature having intended greatness for men' (II, p.176, ch.39). Dorothea does not become a 'great woman' as greatness is measured by the world. Few of us do. The reader is offered no triumph. We are not exonerated from ordinary conditions. Though we share the extraordinariness of the experience of reading *Middlemarch* with its range of control and its insight, we must share equally the foreclosed predicaments of its characters.

Sidney Colvin, in his brilliant essay on the medical and 'symptomatic' nature of *Middlemarch*'s study, points to the disquieting uncertainty in which the book leaves its readers:

In her prelude and conclusion both, she seems to insist upon the design of illustrating the necessary disappointment of a woman's nobler aspirations in a society not made to second noble aspirations in a woman. And that is one of the most burning lessons which any writer could set themselves to illustrate. But then, Dorothea does not suffer in her ideal aspirations from yielding to the pressure of social opinion. She suffers in them from finding, that what she has done, in marrying an old scholar in the face of public opinion, was done under a delusion as to the old scholar's character. 'Exactly', is apparently the author's drift; 'but it is society which so nurtures women that their ideals cannot but be ideals of delusion.' . . .

It is perhaps in pursuance of the same idea that Dorothea's destiny, after Casaubon has died, and she is free from the consequences of a first illusory ideal, is not made very brilliant after all. She cannot be an Antigone or a Theresa. She marries the man of her choice, and bears him children; but we have been made to feel all along that he is hardly worthy of her. There is no sense of triumph in it; there is rather a sense of sadness in a subdued and restricted, if not now a thwarted destiny. (Carroll, 1971, p.337)

Colvin in 1873 is subtly puzzled over the 'moral or intellectual point of view which had dictated so chastened and subdued a conclusion', and so have many readers been ever since. Indeed, a dissatisfaction, either aggressive or melancholy, with the presented outcome of *Middlemarch* has marked some recent feminist criticism, which has seen Dorothea's fate as a reneging on her potential, a capitulation by the writer.

## II

Because so little attention has been paid to George Eliot's relations to the women's movement I shall offer in the first half of this chapter a quite full account of the available material and show ways in which *Middlemarch* took up current questions. George Eliot used the double time-scheme of the novel to create an ironic series of relations to the women's movement I shall offer in the first half of this chapter a quite full account of the available material and show ways in which *Middlemarch* after the passing of the second Reform Bill, 1867. That Bill was the occasion for a vigorous campaign in favour of women's franchise. *The English Woman's Review*, the feminist journal to which George Eliot subscribed, published in January 1867 a powerful article by Barbara Bodichon, entitled 'Authorities and Precedents for Giving the Suffrage to Qualified Women' (pp.63–75). The journal returned to the discussion in its issues of March and July, welcoming the support of John Stuart Mill, who wanted to substitute the word 'person' for 'man' in the Reform Bill. If that word had been changed, some of the history of the next 100 years would have been changed with it.

In the same July issue, 'H.T.' (almost certainly Helen Taylor, Mill's step-daughter) writes one of the most trenchant of the many articles to appear in the journal attacking the idea of separate spheres and separate work possibilities for men and women. She observes that men do 'women's work' in medicine, if we accept the dictum that women's work is defined by its caring and mothering qualities, and that women 'sweep the mud of our crossings' although physical work is usually claimed as men's.

> The truth seems to be that men are, generally speaking, only struck with the unsuitability of work for women when it may lead to profit and honour, and with the unsuitability of work to themselves when there is nothing much worth having to be got by it. *(The Englishwoman's Review*, July 1867, p.231)

Rosamond, with her equivocal name—mystical rose of the world and worldly rose—is a tragic satire on the ideal woman as described in much Victorian writing; in particular, on what constitutes 'women's work' and 'women's influence'. George Eliot had scant patience with the submissive activity of sewing and mending, and even less with that of decorative work such as the chain-work that Rosamond occupies herself with. Embroidery will never 'arouse the dormant faculties of woman' (Pinney, 1963, p.56). Like Elizabeth Barrett Browning in *Aurora Leigh*, which she reviewed enthusiastically in 1857, she saw that what was designated as 'women's work' symbolised their enclosure and their enforced uselessness beyond the private domain, and to a large extent within it:

> By the way,
> The works of women are symbolical,
> We sew, sew, prick our fingers, dull our sight,
> Producing what? A pair of slippers, sir,
> To put on when you're weary—or a stool
> To stumble over and vex you . . . 'curse that stool!'
> Or else at best, a cushion, where you lean
> And sleep, and dream of something we are not
> But would be for your sake. Alas, Alas!
> This hurts most, this that, after all, we are paid
> The worth of our work, perhaps.
>
> (Book I, lines 455-65)

'Woman's influence' was sometimes held to be so powerful a factor that it compensated women for their sequestered role. It was always exercised in private, but supposedly in the most high-minded way. The man is pictured in Mrs Ellis returning from 'the exchange, or the public assembly' to stand corrected 'before the clear eye of woman, as it looked directly to the naked truth' (Ellis, 1838, pp.51-2). The ideal precision attributed to woman's insight by Mrs Ellis and others is mocked in *Middlemarch* in the simplicity with which Rosamond sees straight through every issue to what concerns herself.

Mrs Hugo Reid in her excellently analytical *A Plea for Woman* (1843) had already brought under scrutiny the idea of woman's 'natural sphere'. She argues that the idea of 'female influence', which draws its strength from the mothering metaphor, is both false and corrupting. It is neither a sufficient force nor a safeguard, since the covert element in the concept is that of erotic influence.

> We have still to add a few words to those of our readers who may approve of women taking an interest in politics, but who may think, at the same time, that female influence is a very good substitute for the more direct and straight-forward course of allowing them to express their opinions by voting. We think, that as a substitute for the open and direct method, female influence is a mere phantasm: either it means nothing at all, else it has a bad meaning. It resolves itself into the same kind of influence as is exerted by clear reason and strong argument, whether produced by a man or woman—whether spoken or written; or else it is an instrument which no conscientious woman could justify herself in the use of. (Reid, 1843, p.224)

The notion that women untrained in complexity and constricted by education were endowed with a preter-natural insight is an illusion which George Eliot takes to pieces in her novel. And she does so as much in Dorothea's mistakes as in the limited successes of Rosamond; though Dorothea's shortsightedness, which fortunately unfits her for the arts of worsted work and embroidery, does not prevent her from seeking what is far off, even if its form is blurred or mistaken.

In October 1866, the *Alexandra Magazine* had changed its name to *The English Woman's Review: a Journal of Women's Work*, thus recognising the most insistent focus of feminist concerns by the mid-1860s. For this magazine is in fact continuous with *The English Woman's Journal*, founded in 1857 by Barbara Leigh Smith Bodichon and edited by Bessie Rayner Parkes, which subsequently changed its name to the *Alexandra Magazine* and then, drawing closer again to its original title, to *The English*

*Woman's Review.* The names of Bodichon and Parkes should alert us to the closeness of George Eliot to the milieu of discussion out of which this important journal came. Both Bessie Rayner Parkes and Barbara Bodichon had been friends of Marian Evans since the early 1850s, and Barbara was the most constantly valued friend of her adult life. George Eliot subscribed to the journal from its outset. Barbara Bodichon was a radical but pragmatic feminist. Born outside marriage, she exempted herself from the usual social constraints on women, and used the money that her father gave her on reaching her majority to set up a school and *The English Woman's Journal.* She was one of the founders of Girton College in the 1870s. Her works include *A Brief Summary of the Most Important Laws Concerning Women* (1854) and *Women and Work* (1857). Whereas almost all other discussions of women's education at that time see it in terms of their relationship to men, and many writers praise or dispraise the idea of educating women only in so far as it advances their career as wife and mother, Barbara Bodichon goes much further. She pinpoints the question of education for work in the public world, and sees such training as essential to human independence.

> Every human being should work; no one should owe bread to any but his or her parents ... rational beings ask nothing from their parents save the means of gaining their own livelihood. Fathers have no right to cast the burden of the support of their daughters on other men. It lowers the dignity of women; and tends to prostitution, whether legal or in the streets. As long as fathers regard the sex of a child as a reason why it should not be taught to gain its own bread, so long must women be degraded. Adult women must not be supported by men, if they are to stand as dignified, rational beings before God. (Bodichon, 1857, pp.11–12)

The Society for Promoting the Employment of Women was initiated in 1859 from the same Langham Place offices as *The English Woman's Journal*. Jessie Boucherett, later editor of the journal, organised the society; and the Victoria Women's Printing Press, of which Emily Faithfull was the first manager, printed the journal. So the emphasis on education and work went side by side in theory and in practice, though there were differences within the group about the desirability of full employment for women. Anna Jameson, (the importance of whose writing on symbol and hagiography we have already discussed in analysing *Romola*) was an active worker of an older generation in the women's movement and in this particular group. Already in 1846 she had published two essays, ' "Woman's Mission" and Woman's Position' and 'On the Relative Social Position of Mothers and Governesses', both of which emphasise the 'contradiction' between the position granted to women in society and the 'mission' expected of them:

> To legislate for women as a part of the labouring community, our legislators must first understand what it is in our nature to desire; what it is in our power to perform; what it is in our duty to fulfil. Before you can do us right, you must do away with the wrong. (Jameson, 1846, p.215)

The 'wrong' in her analysis is 'the banishment of woman from her *home*'. Her conclusions are very different from those of the next generation, but this difference is primarily because she is discussing the treatment of working-class as well as middle-class women:

> the poor little female children are sent out at five, nay, at three years old . . . . We cry out about unnatural mothers; but the mother must live,—to live she must work, and make

her children work as soon as they can use their little hands;—no help for it! (Ibid., pp.218–19)

Harriet Martineau, writing on 'Female Industry' in *The Edinburgh Review* (April 1859) declared that 'the era of female industrialism has set in indisputably and irreversibly' but middle-class 'women who must earn their bread are compelled to do it by one of two methods—by the needle or by becoming educators.'

Whereas working-class women enter the labour market and are exploited, middle-class women are excluded from the social organism:

> There is a certain social desertion and loneliness that are even regarded as characteristic of their lot .... The pursuits of men, the movements of industry, the progress of science—in short, the whole ongoings of the outer world, are to her but a phantasmagoria, destitute of reality . . . there is entailed upon her a constant sense of alienation from society.

So writes J.D. Milne in his *Industrial and Social Position of Women* (1857), analysing the patterns of women's labour and the devaluation of women's work. The exclusion of women from the public sphere has, he asserts, the effect of alienating men and women from each other in the middle classes: they meet like puppets, go through a few evolutions, according as the strings of fashion pull.

> Poor Lydgate! or shall I say, Poor Rosamond! Each lived in a world of which the other knew nothing. (I, p.251, ch.16)

Milne's chosen style of analysis is that of the social scientist, not of the natural historian. He attacked the classifications of the 1851 census because 'they appear to be adjusted by some naturalist' not 'by a political economist'. Social scientists were allies of the women's movement and were the first to invite women to speak at public conferences. There are regular reports of social science conventions in *The English Woman's Journal*, as well as articles on 'social science'. *Blackwood's Edinburgh Magazine* commented scathingly on the alliance:

> We believe we are called upon to discuss not 'privileges', but 'rights', for 'social science', we understand, takes as one of its bases the equal rights of woman side by side with man. This startling attitude on the part of the ladies, analogous, we presume, to the uprising of certain oppressed nationalities on the continent of Europe, has at length, we are informed, assumed the definite form of a positive organisation. (*Blackwoods Edinburgh Magazine*, (1861) vol. 90, p.468)

But the 'scientism' and classificatory interest of the male social theorists was distrusted within the women's movement. Bessie Rayner Parkes in her *Essays on Woman's Work* took Milne to task:

> It is not possible to treat a subject like this in a scientific way .... If ... theories respecting masses of men are continually being broken to pieces, how much more impossible is it to argue from abstractions upon the nature of women; for a woman's life is certainly more individual. (Parkes, 1865, pp.219–20)

Bessie Rayner Parkes' conservative individualism emphasises variety.

In the light of such controversy, we begin to understand more precisely the relish with which George Eliot spots ideological difficulty in the Prelude to *Middlemarch*, and joins the discussion, moving the argument in a different direction by linking it to the question of 'Woman's Nature':

> Some have felt that these blundering lives are due to the inconvenient indefiniteness with which the Supreme Power has fashioned the natures of women: if there were one level of feminine incompetence as strict as the ability to count three and no more, the social lot of women might be treated with scientific certitude. Meanwhile the indefiniteness remains, and the limits of variation are really much wider than any one would imagine from the sameness of women's coiffure and the favourite love-stories in prose and verse. (I, pp.2-3, Prelude)

Classification, George Eliot suggests, is not competent to deal with potential. It registers only current organisation; it therefore notes only artificial similarities of the kind that John Stuart Mill saw as induced by women's upbringing and position in society. It can give no account of future transformations, nor sufficiently subtle discriminations. The organisation of *Middlemarch* sets up a tension between classification and individualism.

Bessie Rayner Parkes analyses the problem for sequestered women in terms of finding 'a larger law' for actions:

> Not by bread alone do men or nations live; nor for household uses only can any woman live to whom God has granted means or leisure. Political economy deals with questions of charity, education, state relief of the poor, emigration, and occupation for all classes. None of these things can a woman innocently ignore . . . and in none of them can she move without risk, unless she follows some larger law than the mere pity of the moment. (*Alexandra Magazine* (June 1865) p.373)

This tells precisely on the problem which George Eliot realised in the person of Dorothea Brooke.

*The Alexandra Magazine*, in the same issue, carried an important review of Parkes' book in which the writer claims that opposition to the women's movement became rancorous as soon as they insisted on the right to work. All was well as long as 'the harmony of judicious instruction and advice was all that the public heard through women's words' (*The Alexandra Magazine* p.371). As long as the revival was 'moral and intellectual' and 'women threw their force into benevolence and litera-ture' they were received with 'respect and applause'. But, she asserts, the last ten years have seen a new hostility, 'as if each onward motion were an incursion'. In the movement's new phase money is important:

> It wanted *bread*, and the subject of *earnings* became the burden of its song: when want was actually present, and the need of women in the middle classes, not only of education proper, but of industrial training, and resources in particular, was proclaimed by Miss Parkes, there was a sudden reaction. Men who had approved of the doctrines of the lady writers, when their schemes were mere theories, became impatient when they were reduced to practice, and when plain facts took the place of beautiful visions, they turned on the innocent discoverers, and assailed them with ridicule. (Ibid., p.372)

This intransigent reading of the mid-1860s predicament makes it clear that issues of education and of employ-ment were twinned for women. It was out of them that the franchise movement then achieved mounting intensity.

*Middlemarch* issues out of this debate, though it is not confined to it. It is about work and the right to work, about the need to discover a vocation which will satisfy the whole self and to be educated to undertake it. This theme is explored principally in Lydgate and in Dorothea and the novel nicely judges their different problems. *Middlemarch* is about false education, both of women and of men. In its narrative order it puts taxonomy under pressure as it first classifies, and then discovers more and more subtle and vital differences. The novel is most particularly concerned with the problems of women excluded from work and from fulfilling activity, sequestered by their education. *The English Woman's Journal* debates the problem of philanthropic voluntary work and questions whether middle-class women should work without wages. It looks too at 'model cottages', and at the intellectual exclusion of women.

> For to Dorothea, after that toy-box history of the world adapted to young ladies which had made the chief part of her education, Mr Casaubon's talk about his great book was full of new vistas. (I, p.128, ch.10)

Celia plays ' "an air with variations", a small kind of tinkling which symbolised the aesthetic part of the young ladies' education' (I, p.63, ch.5).

## III

George Eliot sets her novel nearly 40 years before the period in which it is written. By this stroke she is able to explore a series of connections and analogies between present and past, and use the unwritten period between. In one sense, the whole period of the growth of the women's movement is excluded from the novel. In another, as narrative discourse and as reader's retrospect, it becomes the matter of the novel's irony and of its melancholy idealism.

One of the most striking examples of intertextuality in *Middlemarch* occurs in relation to the 'stupendous fragmentariness' of Rome's meaning for Dorothea which 'heightened the dream-like strangeness of her bridal life'.

> She had been led through the best galleries, had been taken to the chief points of view, had been shown the greatest ruins and the most glorious churches, and she had ended by oftenest choosing to drive out to the Campagna where she could feel alone with the earth and sky, away from the oppressive masquerade of ages, in which her own life too seemed to become a masque with enigmatical costumes. (I, p. 296, ch. 20)

In the introductory essay in *Essays on Woman's Work* (1865) Bessie Rayner Parkes describes her experience in visiting Rome at a time when she had been 'intensely engaged in work pertaining to the *English Woman's Journal*'. Her habitual work assumed 'the likeness of a dream': 'There was a world beyond the mountains, a world of activities and reforms; but its murmur was here unheard' (Parkes, 1865, p. 11). 'Sitting high up amidst the gigantic ruins, and looking out over the domes and towers on to the broad gray sweeps of the Campagna' her mind 'reverted to the home work, to the ferment of thought and feeling' (Ibid., p. 12). She wonders how to place all that life in relation to 'the vastness of Rome, whose history embraces many ages of time, and three great empires of faith'. Then Bessie Rayner Parkes has a vision:

> As I looked over this immense expanse, there suddenly rose before my mind a vision of the countless multitude of women who have lived and died. Women of many nations, and of many faiths: Etruscans, adorned with fine gold, very

proud in their ancient lineage, allied both to Egypt and to Greece; Romans of the regal, the republican, and the imperial times, women who have lived under the most despotic and the most just laws, and who were virtuous and respected under the first epoch, and debased and degraded at the very time when they had secured so much of freedom. Then I thought of the early Christian women, saints, virgins, and martyrs; of the armies of nuns whose rule had gone forth from Rome, and of hundreds still busy within its walls, praying, teaching, or tending the sick; of women who were brave in the old times, and feared neither the axe, nor the stake, nor the hungry war of beasts in that very Colosseum which lifted its ruined arches before me in the red radiance. One half of the great nations of antiquity, one half of the church militant,—these were women. (Ibid., 13–14)

This vision of sisterhood, of the 'countless multitude of women' living under varying conditions, 'of saints, virgins, and martyrs', comforts her and makes her accept political relativism and a sense of individuals' survival: 'I felt how partial are the efforts of any particular nation in the solving of moral questions which have found, from age to age, some sort of practical solution in a million homes' (ibid.).

Rayner Parkes finds a lyrical assuaging in the connections between 'unhistoric' women. But Dorothea Brooke is not part of the Langham Place group, not part of any sisterhood, and remains unacquainted with the writing on myths of women by Anna Jameson. Nor can she be Saint Theresa or Saint Dorothea. She is one of those millions seeking, and failing to find, 'some sort of practical solution' of moral questions in her home. She has no alternative discourse with which to make sense of her experience. To her, Rome is 'an oppressive masquerade of ages'. It is to her friends in the women's movement particularly that George Eliot directs her commentary here, conceiving 'one more historical contrast'.

> To those who have looked at Rome with the quickening power of a knowledge which *breathes a growing soul into all historic shapes, and traces out the suppressed transitions which unite all contrasts*, Rome may still be the spiritual centre and interpreter of the world. But let them conceive one more historical contrast: the gigantic broken revelations of that Imperial and Papal city thrust abruptly on the notions of a girl who had been brought up in English and Swiss Puritanism, fed on meagre Protestant histories and on art chiefly of the hand-screen sort; a girl whose ardent nature turned all her small allowance of knowledge into principles, fusing her actions into their mould, and whose quick emotions gave the most abstract things the quality of a pleasure or a pain; a girl who had lately become a wife, and from the enthusiastic acceptance of untried duty found herself plunged in tumultuous preoccupation with her personal lot. The weight of unintelligible Rome might lie easily on bright nymphs to whom it formed a background for the brilliant picnic of Anglo-foreign society; but Dorothea had no such defence against deep impressions. (I, p.296, ch.20; emphasis added)

Neither Dorothea nor Bessie is a 'bright nymph', but George Eliot, in this sub-text, discerns how raised consciousness may reassure the initiated, and the community of activists may thus lose sight of the isolation of those they seek to serve. It has been suggested that Barbara Bodichon was a model for Dorothea. Perhaps, rather, Bessie Parkes and Barbara Bodichon provided models of Dorothea's possibilities, and measures of her curtailment. Their achievement and their muddles, particularly those of Bessie, offer a subtle register upon which to place Dorothea: Dorothea finds no community of like-minded women.

> Here and there a cygnet is reared uneasily among the ducklings in the brown pond, and never finds the living stream in fellowship with its own oary-footed kind. *Here and there is born a Saint Theresa, foundress of nothing* whose loving heart-beats and sobs after an unattained goodness tremble off and are dispersed among hindrances, instead of centering in some long-recognizable deed. (I, p.3, Prelude: emphasis added)

## *IV*

The period in which George Eliot grew to adulthood was one which saw an increasing number of studies of the condition of women, some of which had outcome in action. In the 1840s the emphasis in England was on realising fully the special moral influence of women. The route towards liberation, such as it was, was still based on their mothering role. As Françoise Basch formulates it:

> Any activity deriving from woman's specific role of mother, exercising an ennobling and purifying influence in the natural framework of her family, alleviating suffering and sacrificing herself to others, was recognized as legitimate. (Basch, 1974, p.115)

This role could be extended 'to encompass society at large, seen now as a vast family'. Bonnie Zimmerman remarks,

> Shattering the dichotomy of home and world was one way to increase power in the nineteenth century. Extending the

home to *encompass* the world was another, and far more common, way. (Zimmerman, 1980, p.91)

Works such as the anonymous *Woman's Rights and Duties* took a somewhat more militant line than that of Louis Aimé-Martin, *The Education of Mothers of Families; or The Civilization of The Human Race by Women* (1842). Reading Martin 'electrified' the young Marian Evans. She had already read Ellis's *Woman's Mission*, the work whose contradictory message is attacked by Anna Jameson in ' "Woman's Mission" and Woman's Position' (1846). Sydney Owenson Morgan's *Woman and Her Master* (1840) looked in historical terms at the treatment of women by men; Mrs Hugo Reid wrote *A Plea for Woman: being a vindication of the importance and extent of her natural sphere of action,* (1843). As Anna Jameson commented, 'The press has lately teemed with works treating of the condition, the destiny, the duties of women .... The theme, however treated, is one of the themes of the day' (1846, pp.15–16). Catchpenny titles, as well as serious works, continued to teem through the 1850s, like Steven Fullom's *The History of Woman, and her Connexion with Religion, Civilization and Domestic Manners, From the Earliest Period* (1855) which Marian Evans/George Eliot denounced in the *Westminster Review* in 1855.

But despite the degree of discussion in the 1840s and 1850s, the state of legislation concerning women was still primitive:

> Man's legislation for woman has hitherto been like English legislation for Ireland: it has been without sympathy; without the recognition of equality; without a comprehension of certain innate differences. (Ibid., pp.214–15)

The connection with oppressed races, with 'operatives'

and with slaves, were all essential to the vocabulary of Victorian feminism. The fascination in George Eliot's novels and poems with gypsies and Jews—races excluded from the dominating culture—also owes something to this discourse. Fedalma in *The Spanish Gypsy* compresses the figure of the woman trapped between dominant culture and tribal descent and oppressed by both.

The state of legislation, about property rights and about divorce, held women in a state of dependency. This was completed by their lack of education and their economic dependence on the home either of husband or father. The author of *Woman's Rights and Duties* had compared the enforced fecklessness of women and slaves. If they sustained 'natural buoyancy of spirit it was assumed that slaves' condition was good enough. The same shallow view is sometimes taken of the condition of women.' But 'the want of liberty destroys all motives for exertion.' Barbara Bodichon, travelling through Mississippi in 1858, writes ironically of the emphasis given to religious differences:

> To believe in transubstantiation or the divinity of the Virgin is not so perverting to the mind as to believe that women have no rights to full development of all their faculties and exercise of all their powers, to believe that men have rights over women, and as fathers to exercise those pretended rights over daughters, as husbands exercising those rights over wives. Every day men acting on this false belief destroy their perception of justice, blunt their moral nature, so injure their consciences that they lose the power to perceive the highest and purest attributes of God. Slavery is a greater injustice, but it is allied to the injustice to women so closely that I cannot see one without thinking of the other and feeling how soon slavery would be destroyed if right opinions were entertained upon the other question. (Bodichon, ed. Reed, 1972, p.63)

In *Felix Holt*, and even more in *Daniel Deronda*, George Eliot explores the condition of women, apparently at ease, living privileged lives, and yet atrophied by their condition of slavery. Mrs Transome, Mrs Glasher and Gwendolen all share this imagery. In *Middlemarch* Rosamond Vincy is a woman entrapped so completely that she is hardly aware of it, so smoothly does her compliance fit. And that 'type of woman' most traps men into mutual delusion:

> Lydgate thought that after all his wild mistakes and absurd credulity, he had found perfect womanhood—felt as if already breathed upon by exquisite wedded affection such as would be bestowed by an accomplished creature who venerated his high musings and momentous labours and would never interfere with them; who would create order in the home and accounts with still magic, yet kept her fingers ready to touch the lute and transform life into romance at any moment; who was instructed to the true womanly limit and not a hair's-breadth beyond—docile, therefore, and ready to carry out behests which came from beyond that limit. (II, pp.120–1, ch.36)

When in 1855 Barbara Bodichon drew up a petition in support of the Married Women's Property Bill, she wrote that the aim of the Bill was 'that in entering the state of marriage, they no longer pass from freedom into the condition of a slave' (Burton, 1949, p.71). George Eliot signed this petition and distributed sheets for it. Also in 1855 there was a commission on the law of mortmain. 'The Dead Hand' in *Middlemarch*, as Book V is titled, refers to 'mortmain': the impress of Mr Casaubon's will on Dorothea's subsequent life and of Featherstone's on that of Mary Garth and Fred Vincy.

Throughout her writing career, George Eliot was notably interested in legal problems. She increasingly researched not only the immediate effects on women's position, but also the ideological assumptions embedded in the laws of inheritance and of kin. The patriarchal nature of law became clearer with the increase in historical and anthropological studies of women's position. As George Eliot worked through Lecky's *History of European Morals* she particularly noted such material. This concern links her with the pressing interests of her friends active in the women's movement. Divorce, child custody, married women's property rights—all figure constantly in *The English Woman's Journal*.

George Eliot uses the pivot of the unwritten years in *Middlemarch*—the years between setting and composition —to register some changes in women's circumstances, but rather small change in the actual conditions of women's lives. One of the sad speculative movements of the book is to bring into question the extent to which any real enfranchisement has been achieved between 1830 and 1870.

In George Eliot's novels 'independence' implies money, but money does not guarantee independence. Dorothea is beset by the problems of her money and by her ignorance of how best to use it. She asks Casaubon to compensate Ladislaw for the exclusion of his grandmother from her rights of inheritance. She wants to use her money wisely. At the end of the book she leaves behind Casaubon's money, which has become loaded with his jealous will. Mary Garth alone maintains independence without money, and her integrity is rescued and pastoralised by the novel's events, which conspire to free her from the consequences of her refusal to connive with Featherstone. Maggie Tulliver's predicament was in part that her independence of mind was not matched by independent means: much of the narrative, after all, is concerned with the drop in her family's fortunes. Gwendolen goes into marriage with Grandcourt as a way of recouping her family funds and providing for her mother.

Marrying for money, when the alternative is to live in the woman's land of governessing, seamstressing, or even aimless genteel poverty, is a real alternative. It may give a woman some form of independence, a household to manage, funds to dispense, a career of a kind. The forlorn passivity of the unmarried daughter, even when her parents are alive, was a constant theme of Victorian feminist writing. If only, say the Shirreff sisters, or Emily Faithfull, or Barbara Bodichon, women were educated in such a way that they could earn their own living and achieve independence. Idleness eats away vitality or leaves it ricocheting without control. So the campaigns for education, work and independent property rights are very closely and coherently connected.

In *Middlemarch* education and money 'greatly determine' the characters, and George Eliot takes as her central topic the unfit preparation of women for life's opportunities. This is a theme as crucial for understanding Rosamond as it is for understanding Dorothea.

The obverse of the same problem is shown in the experience of Lydgate. Lydgate is imaginative in relation to science, tender in his impulses, and yet utterly untrained to treat with analytical seriousness the emotional business of life. The emphasis on women's 'special province' of feeling is shown to disable even those men talented in emotion. Lydgate has never been led to evaluate his own ignorance. Casaubon—a great believer in the separate spheres principle—cannot experience emotion except as fear and anger.

Will Ladislaw, son of two generations of rebellious women, is shown as lucid about his own feelings and responsive to women. He is not shut up in his own masculinity. He is not much oppressed by guilt. His failure for a long time to find a role in the world sets him alongside women's experience. He is outside the educational hegemony. His problem is to find a use for himself. His attachment to Dorothea is sound and yet for much of the book a little dilettante, like his opinions. It thrives on delicacy and distance, on the edge of commitment. It is hard for him, after all, to *do* anything, except gently to seduce her to criticise her husband. He feels grandeur, though he does not feel grandly. It is that quality of the aspirant which distinguishes him. He hopes for much. He delights in many things. He is kin to women, not polarised against them. Ladislaw's position, outside money inheritance, sharing the awkward financial dependency more often associated with women, does have the effect of reinforcing his feminisation. It also shows that not only women suffer from dependency and powerlessness. At the same time, Will is much freer than a woman in an equivalent position would be—and that is a pointer to another of his uses. He exactly focuses what is peculiar to women's predicament by sharing many of their conditions, and yet living a liberated life. This liberation depends upon his being a man, with freedom to travel, to live where he will, and to make his own friends.

Throughout *Middlemarch* the multiple points of comparison and divergence between characters in the text enable George Eliot to draw more and more exactly the focus of her experiments.

Dorothea finds it hard to distinguish between love and learning: this is a problem which bears particularly hard on women. The mentor–pupil relationship in its male–female form presents the man as teacher and the woman as pupil. The pattern traditionally extends across intellectual and sexual experience. Men teach

women sexually and intellectually. To Dorothea, passion and knowledge are identified. She seeks to *know*
more than her meagre education has so far allowed her,
and thereby to *do* more than her society designates as
appropriate to her. At the beginning of the book,
Casaubon is irradiated for her by the light of his
imagined knowledge. His great project suggests a world
of interconnection and exploration which satisfies her
heart. Dorothea clearly figures partly as a chastened re-
reading of the writer's own early experience; in
particular, her attraction to learned older men who
seemed to offer access to an intensified world of ideas. In
her relationship with Herbert Spencer, Marian Evans
had been forced to the point of understanding that the
power of intellectual synthesis does not guarantee
emotional power or sexual feeling.

But Dorothea is not utterly wrong about Casaubon.
He does represent a way out of safety. She needs risks as
well as usefulness and her enclosed environment has not
taught her to recognise worse imprisonment. Casaubon's
devoted commitment to a large intellectual project,
though it has turned into a search which simplifies all
complexity back into a single form, does yet represent an
aspiration which remains with Dorothea throughout the work. The proper and liberating task proves in
the course of the book to be that of making connections,
not seeking origins. So she learns to do without the
masculine as father. She grows out of her belief that
men father knowledge, are its origin and its guardian:
'The really delightful marriage must be that where your
husband was a sort of father, and could teach you even
Hebrew, if you wished it' (I, p.12, ch.1). She is herself an
orphan and by the death of Casaubon is released from
the oppressive demands of another 'sort of father'.

Her attraction to Will grows through the play of spirit

Her attraction to Will grows through the play of spirit and learning between them: they teach each other. He frees her from desiring martyrdom; she gives him a great project. The rapidity of interconnection in their conversation is reinforced by the narrative discourse; spontaneity and danger, innovation and scepticism, are all represented in the dialogues at Rome. The work beautifully records the extent to which falling in love *is* conversation, the passionate discovery and exchange of meanings. Will is, as Mr Brooke sagely remarks, 'a kind of Shelley', absolutely at home in the world of ideas, yet uncertain how to use this knowledge. He and Dorothea educate each other, abandoning the model of mentor and pupil as a kind of father and daughter. The book itself resists the usual punitive outcome for lovers who educate each other which is shown in the stories of Francesca and Paulo, Abelard and Heloise, Julie and St Preux.

But lovers cannot be relied on as educators. Institutions are essential. One of the principal areas in which it was possible to doubt improvement between 1830 and 1870 was in the nature of women's education. In the 1860s the *Alexandra Magazine* emphasised the need for women to take part in examinations, because they would otherwise never be tested or qualified alongside men. In an article on 'A Comparison between the Education of Girls in France and England' we find that

> Englishwomen have now the advantages of the extended education desired for them; they do sympathize largely in the progress of the world of ideas, but the superficial nature of the instruction which they receive, is making itself felt in every matter in which they are concerned. (*The Alexandra Magazine*, March 1865, p.133)

The unsympathetic nature of women's education and

training had been commented on by the Shirreff sisters in *Thoughts on Self-Culture*:

> In general, there has been everything to thwart and nothing to encourage in women the desire to study. The more pompous enumeiation of school-room learning in the present day makes no real difference in this respect; in that chaos of laborious trifling, it would be vain to expect that the mind should be trained to any serious method of study; and, therefore, when a woman becomes convinced of the value of mental pursuits, and desires to cultivate them, she is at a loss to know how or what to begin; she is aware how superficial is all her previously acquired information, but how to learn better, and what to seek first, are points concerning which she feels perplexed and helpless. (Shirreff, 1854, p.262)

The situation described—the sense of ineffectual striving and discouragement—is close to that more metaphorically represented for Dorothea:

> For a long while she had been oppressed by the indefiniteness which hung in her mind, like a thick summer haze, over all her desire to make her life greatly effective. What could she do, what ought she to do?—she, hardly more than a budding woman, but yet with an active conscience and a great mental need, not to be satisfied by a girlish instruction comparable to the nibblings and judgments of a discursive mouse. (I, p.39, ch.3)

Immediately after, the narrative condenses imagery which thrives on allusions beyond Dorothea's reach:

> The intensity of her religious disposition, the coercion it exercised over her life, was but one aspect of a nature altogether ardent, theoretic, and intellectually consequent: and with such a nature struggling in the bands of a narrow

teaching, hemmed in by a social life which seemed nothing but a labyrinth of petty courses, a walled-in maze of small paths that led no whither, the outcome was sure to strike others as at once exaggeration and inconsistency. (Ibid.)

The allusion to Blake's infant in the *Songs of Experience* summons a primal energy imprisoned by society and kin: part of the poignant intensification lies in the awareness that Dorothea cannot cross the transition into the metaphors of the commentary not because of any lack of intelligence, but because of a lack of education. Labyrinths have become petty garden mazes. Mr Brooke, with his own delightfully unreconstructed eclecticism, speaks out frankly the assumptions about women which result in such frittering of potentiality:

'But there is a lightness about the feminine mind—a touch and go—music, the fine arts, that kind of thing—they should study those up to a certain point, women should; but in a light way, you know'. (I, p.94, ch.7)

The implicit comparison between conditions in the 1830s and 70s is used to show not how much things have improved, but how little.

In *Aurora Leigh* (1857) Elizabeth Barrett Browning describes a relatively thoroughgoing girl's education:

I learnt my complement of classic French
(Kept pure of Balzac and neologism)
And German also, since she liked a range
Of liberal education,—tongues, not books.
I learnt a little algebra, a little
Of the mathematics,—brushed with extreme flounce
The circle of the sciences, because
She disliked women who are frivolous.
(Book I, lines 399–405)

All this was to prepare her to be a wife of the kind that would exactly have suited Mr Casaubon:

> I read a score of books on womanhood
> To prove, if women do not think at all,
> They may teach thinking, (to a maiden aunt
> Or else the author)—books demonstrating
> Their right of comprehending husband's talk
> When not too deep, and even of answering
> With pretty 'may it please you,' or 'so it is,'—
> Their rapid insight and fine aptitude,
> Particular worth and general missionariness,
> As long as they keep quiet by the fire
> And never say 'no' when the world says 'ay',
> For that is fatal,—their angelic reach
> Of virtue, chiefly used to sit and darn,
> And fatten household sinners,—their, in brief,
> Potential faculty in everything
> Of abdicating power in it.
>
> (Book I, lines 426–41)

In her enthusiastic review of *Aurora Leigh* in 1857, George Eliot quoted approvingly another such passage in which Aurora refuses 'To show a pretty spirit, chiefly admired/Because true action is impossible'. (*Westminster Review*, 67, 1857, p.308)

In the *Report on the Committee of Council* (1869–70) Mr Allington reports:

> Girls fail much more frequently than boys in all subjects and in all standards. It does not necessarily follow that they are inferior to boys in capacity, but as a matter of fact, owing partly to previous neglect and partly to the comparative indifference with which even sensible parents still regard the education of their daughters, the girls ... are as a rule far below the boys in attainments. (Grey, 1871, p.19)

Maria Grey, in *The Education of Women*, comments in a

style which exactly describes the outcome of Rosamond's
lady-like education:

> They are *not* educated to be wives, but to get husbands. They
> are *not* educated to be mothers; if they were, they would
> require and obtain the highest education that could be
> given, in order to fit them for the highest duties a human
> being can perform. They are *not* educated to be the
> mistresses of households; if they were, their judgment
> would be as sedulously trained, habits of method and
> accuracy as carefully formed, as they are now neglected.
> They would not give, as Mr Bryce calculates, 5,520 hours of
> their school life to music against 640 to arithmetic; and
> social and political economy, which are scarcely thought of
> in their course of instruction now, would take the foremost
> place in it. (Ibid., p.20)

Joshua Fitch, among the most enlightened of Victorian
workers for women's education, wrote in his report to
the Schools Inquiry Commission an account of intellectual estrangement in marriage which runs alongside
that of Lydgate and Rosamond:

> It would not be difficult to point to thousands of instances of
> men who have started in life with a love of knowledge and
> with a determination to master at least some department of
> honourable thought or inquiry; yet who have gradually
> sunk into habits of mental indolence, have allowed all their
> great aims to fade out of view, and have become content
> with the reading supplied by Mudie and the newspapers,
> simply from a dread of isolation. . . . There is no hope for the
> middle classes, until the range of topics which they care
> about includes something more than money making,
> religious controversies, and ephemeral politics. (Ibid., 56–7)

Starting from this relativist position of considering
women in relation to men's good he reaches a position

still rare, then and since, of asserting a woman's right to knowledge:

> When they come to consider this, they will set as great a value on intellectual power or literary taste when they are put forth by a girl as by a boy; and they will feel that the true measure of a woman's right to knowledge is her capacity for receiving it, and not any theories of ours, as to what she is fit for or what use she is likely to make of it. (Ibid.)

These are some of the predicaments that George Eliot enters in *Middlemarch*: Lydgate's 'allowing his great aims to fade out of view'; Rosamond 'being from morning till night her own standard of a perfect lady' (I, p.253, ch.16); Dorothea's sense of the 'chaos of laborious trifling . . . at a loss to know how or where to begin', misinterpreting Mr Casaubon as a possible way out of her 'walled-in maze of small paths that led no whither' (p.39). The mind of the young woman 'bewildered and overcome . . . can neither understand its own wants, nor frame a method to meet them' (Shirreff, 1854; p.263).

George Eliot's piercing sarcasm in the first books of *Middlemarch* works at the expense of the 1870s reader's easy developmental assumption of distance from the material of 1830s life. How far have things changed? The comments of her concerned contemporaries show how little. Although conditions have changed again, modern readers are likely to recognise a process of attrition and exclusion in the predicaments of Rosamond and of Dorothea, even of Mary Garth, which is still a crucial concern for all those concerned with the education of women and of men in the present day.

George Eliot, then, did engage with issues vital in the life of the women's movement. The kind of comment we often encounter that 'she always sought to be free of any close involvement with the feminist movement of her time either in life or in literature' (Miles, 1974; p.52) is simply not true. Nor is Ellen Moers' flat assertion that George Eliot was 'no feminist' to be accepted. We do not need to convert her into a radical feminist: it would be pointless to pretend to do so. What is demonstrable is that she was intimately familiar with the current writing and actions of the women's movement and that in *Middlemarch* particularly, she brooded on the curtailment of women's lives in terms drawn from that movement and in sympathy with it.

## V

But uncertainty does remain. Where precisely *did* George Eliot stand on the women's movement and women's rights? Did she, in Dorothea, praise women's 'potential faculty in everything of abdicating power in it'? (*Aurora Leigh*). She is not, as Zelda Austen makes clear, a woman writer who writes solely 'about women from a woman's point of view, and, more narrowly, about liberated women from a liberated woman's point of view' (Austen, 1976, p.556). So far as her life went, we know that although she was a subscriber to the *English Woman's Journal* she was never a contributor, and that Bessie Rayner Parkes grudged her refusal to write for them. Her life will not take us all the way into her writing. Up to now in this chapter I have been indicating ways in which her writing engaged with the vocabulary and the ideas of the women's movement, and the extent to which she concurred with Barbara Bodichon's position. Later in this chapter I shall consider an issue which may allow us to reach further. This is the function of metaphor and of organisation in extending *Middlemarch's* questioning of history and of 'natural law'.

It would be a mistake to accept George Eliot's 'realism' as a purely descriptive or a socially confirming method, or to interpret *Middlemarch* solely in terms of its empirical relations to current writing and events. But I hope I have already demonstrated the speculative energy that went into her reading and interpretation, an energy which drives her out into *possibilities*, an enterprise akin to that oft-quoted passage on Lydgate's imagination with its significant and momentary doubling of the sense of 'relation' as relationship and narrative: 'he was enamoured of that arduous invention which is the very eye of research, provisionally framing its object and correcting it to more and more exactness of relation' (I, p.249, ch.16) Possibilities are recognised as coherence of relations.

Before we leave the biographical question of that figure 'George Eliot', so authoritatively inscribed on the title-page and bearing so tortuous, yet ungainsayable, a relationship to Mrs Lewes, let us consider the evidence of the life and letters for what light they may cast on unresolved questions of allegiance and default.

Almost every one of the women with whom George Eliot was intimate from the mid-1850s was actively involved in the women's movement. One such was Clementia Doughty (Mrs Peter Taylor), a worker for women's suffrage; another less active was the positivist Maria Bury (Mrs Richard Congreve). Bessie Rayner Parkes and Barbara Bodichon we have already discussed. Edith Simcox we shall come to. When periods of estrangement with Barbara came,—as they will come in long relationships—they were over questions other than the women's movement: issues such as personal immortality and George Eliot's determined abandonment of the idea. The socially more daring and active Barbara Bodichon writes to Bessie in 1861:

Since Pater's death the hopelessness of life without immortality has made me quite lean off from Marian . . . fond as I am of her. . . . I told Marian if I felt *convinced* as she professes to be of *utter annihilation*, I should not have power to live for this little scrap of life'. (Bessie Rayner Parkes, V, 178, MS, Girton)

Courage takes diverse forms. George Eliot's own affirmed lifestyle, living unmarried with a still-married man, meant that it was probably inevitable that all her close women friends should be active in the women's movement, since they were the only ones who would visit her and accept her fully. Only in her late years did her home become a fashionable intellectual centre; and even then most visitors were men. Bessie Rayner Parkes describes a visit where she found Marian Lewes surrounded by men and felt her relief at the arrival of women. We should not condescendingly assume that Bessie was mistaken.

One of the most impressively courageous workers for women's rights among George Eliot's intimates was Edith Simcox, the young and learned woman who fell in love with George Eliot during the last years of her life. Edith Simcox has been harshly treated by biographers of George Eliot. By extracting for quotation from her journal only those passages which have bearing on George Eliot, she has been transformed into a lap-dog. Her lesbianism has been a source of acute unease to writers who have misread as 'sentimental effusion' what are often courageous statements of attachment and self-recognition. Edith Simcox was an international socialist and on the national committee of the first International Working Men's Association. She founded the first trade union for women, and was one of the first two women delegates at the Trades Union Congress. She organised a collective of women workers in the exploited clothing trade, hence the title of her journal 'Autobiography of a Shirtmaker'. She was an excellent Germanist, wrote a philosophical work on *Natural Law* (1877), and a perceptive essay on *Middlemarch*.

Because she is pictured only at George Eliot's feet, it is insufficiently understood how far her passion for George Eliot and for her writing liberated Edith Simcox into action. In the midst of a vivid account of a packed women workers' meeting and of the conditions in which they work, she comments, 'It is very mysterious the way all my mental energies are stimulated by a touch from her.' On another Sunday she leaves George Eliot, attends the 'Shirtmakers' Committee', then, 'I walked home—crossing Hyde Park for the first time in the dark.' This is testimony to set over-against the debilitating view of Lynn Linton, or the oppressed awareness of George Eliot's life and writing which weighs on Mrs Oliphant. Neither Mrs Linton nor Mrs Oliphant were in sympathy with the women's movement. The people to whom George Eliot offered energy prove almost to a woman to have been so. How then do we interpret her peripheral and equivocal role?

So far as her own life went there was one obvious tactical reason why it might be sound sense for George Eliot to remain a counsellor and friend behind the scenes. Her 'irregular' life might jeopardise more than it gained for the movement if she were an open and active supporter. This reason may not suffice, but it should not be discounted. It is very easy from our point of advantage to underestimate the enormous step George Eliot took in committing herself to a relationship which put her outside society. It made it necessary for her to renegotiate every other relationship. Some of the most valued, like that with her brother, foundered.

Law-breaking may make us law-abiding. We carefully

conform in order to make room for sustained resistance. (It will be remembered that what her brother Isaac blamed her for was her 'secrecy'.) The massive caution of her later behaviour and expressions of opinion should be seen in the light of this doubling. The 'studied restraint' and counteractive 'temperament' which Lynn Linton described with jealous shrewdness issued from 'her endeavour to harmonise two irreconcilables—to be at once conventional and insurgent' (Linton, 1899, p.97).

George Eliot herself, late in life, claimed that her function was 'that of the *aesthetic*, not the doctrinal teacher .... If I had taken a contrary decision, I should not have remained silent till now' (Haight, 1956, p.44). She is replying to Mrs Peter Taylor's request to her to speak out, though we do not know on what subject. The heaviness of statement in such letters lies oddly alongside the more complicated activity of the fiction. When in this letter she speaks of her enterprise as 'the rousing of the nobler emotions, which make mankind desire the social right', the effect is altogether less convincing than that which we encounter as reading process in the novels. The experience of relation, delay, pain, resolve, irresolution, that we participate in as readers, is both more engrossing and more disquieting than this passage suggests. But George Eliot correctly emphasises the *affective* nature of her fiction and the grounding of its claims to social action in that quality.

No commentary can replicate or enlarge, for example, the effect of Chapter 74 of *Middlemarch* in which Mrs Bulstrode sets out to discover what has happened to her husband by visiting her friends, at last hears the truth from her brother, and at the chapter's end moves to her husband's side. We enter experience here through the play of dialogue, wit, free indirect discourse, metaphor, recounting, unsaid statement. That is, we enter experience not only alongside the characters but *as reading*. The chapter may move us to tears because the language allows us 'to conceive with that distinctness which is no longer reflection but feeling—an idea wrought back to the directness of sense, like the solidity of objects' (I, p.323, ch.21). The impossibility of *foreseeing* either Mrs Bulstrode's behaviour, or our experience, as readers, bears out George Eliot's claim that her best work is done in silence, the silence of writing.

Within that silence, insurgence and conformity can both take their place. Dorothea is not obliged to call upon the divorce laws: Casaubon conveniently dies. But her resistance to him remains, so that she is even driven to write him a letter after his death explaining that she cannot bind herself to complete his project. In an early review Marian Evans had noted sardonically that in novels 'deaths always happen thus opportunely' (*Westminster Review*, 67, 1857, pp.306–10). In *Middlemarch* the 'opportuneness' of death is employed in the figure of Casaubon; it is sceptically surveyed as the central knot of the plot in the death of Raffles (so opportune for Bulstrode, so disbelieved in by the community who know that such opportune deaths happen only in romances); while in the subsequent life of Lydgate no release is offered, until the sad opportuneness of his own early death releases Rosamond into a wealthy second marriage when she 'often spoke of her happiness as "a reward" ' (II, p.460, Finale). This complicated use of 'opportune' death marks George Eliot's particular quality as a writer. The novels' enabling scepticism towards fictional and social orders never diminishes strong feeling. But the same mixture of feeling and scepticism made it difficult, perhaps increasingly so, for her to feel much confidence in the power of specific social measures to rectify women's lot. In the Cabinet edition she removed sentences from the Finale which include: 'society smiled ... on modes of education which make a woman's knowledge another name for motley ignorance—on rules of conduct which are in flat contradiction with its own loudly-asserted beliefs'.

Did she feel that the overdetermination of women's predicament made any such local symptoms inadequate as explanation, and therefore too comforting to the reader? Or had she lost faith in the potential for change of the women's movement? I take the former view, but I do not think that we can look for a single position. She needed and sustained contradiction, and, even more multiplied positions than contradiction.

The "nature of women" troubled her as an idea, and as an experience, throughout her life. We have seen how the image of the mother as originator moves through her relationship to her own writing. She wrote in 1869 that she 'profoundly rejoiced that I never brought a child into the world', and yet is 'conscious of having an unused stock of motherly tenderness'. She wrote admiringly to Harriet Beecher Stowe: 'you have had longer experience than I as a writer, and fuller experience as a woman, since you have borne children and know the mother's history from the beginning.' The sense of 'the mother's history' as a narrative reserved from her and to be discovered only laboriously, only enigmatically as art, fuels much of the intensity of *Daniel Deronda* where the characters must seek absent mothers, as Deronda and Mirah do; or learn to live with mothers who cling to and threaten them, as Gwendolen must with her own mother and with Mrs Glasher.

George Eliot was writing in a period before women could readily control their own fertility. Childbearing, therefore, peculiarly marks women and opposes them to men. We have seen how the problem of generalising the

mothering role across society, and across class, preoccupied the women's movement and was the source of
many divisions within it. It is in the light of such
arguments that we should read George Eliot's letter to
John Morley, written while she was working on
*Middlemarch*. Morley was at the time publishing articles
in *The Fortnightly* supporting the movement for women's
franchise and, in this month of May, John Stuart Mill
moved an amendment to Gladstone's Reform Bill to
permit women to vote:

> Your attitude in relation to Female Enfranchisement seems
> to be very nearly mine. If I were called on to act in the
> matter, I would certainly not oppose any plan which held
> out any reasonable promise of tending to establish as far as
> possible an equivalence of advantages for the two sexes, as
> to education and the possibilities of free development. I fear
> you may have misunderstood something I said the other
> evening about nature. I never meant to urge the 'intention
> of Nature' argument, which is to me a pitiable fallacy. I mean
> that as a fact of mere zoological evolution, woman seems to
> me to have the worse share in existence. But for that very
> reason I would the more contend that in the moral evolution
> we have 'an art which does mend nature'—an art which
> 'itself is nature'. (Haight, 1978, VIII, p.402)

George Eliot denies the 'intention of Nature' argument,
which argues that women's current role is immutable
and fixed by nature, but affirms that in terms of zoology
(their childbearing?) women have the worse share. Yet,
she declares, quoting *The Winter's Tale* with its fructifying
argument that the discoveries of culture (including the
'artificial') are aspects of the natural order which is thus
open to change, women have 'an art which does mend
nature'.

In 'Armgart' four years later, the contrary possibilities
of art and nature are divided differently. Armgart
declares:

> I am an artist by my birth—
> By the same warrant that I am a woman: . . .
> I need not crush myself within a mould
> Of theory called Nature: I have room
> To breathe and grow unstunted.
>
> *(Poems,* p.98)

But that is possible to Armgart only because of her exceptionalness. Once her splendid voice is gone,she finds herself trapped in the common lot of disregarded women, though she recovers herself through teaching, not through marriage and children. The letter paragraph ends thus:

> It is the function of love in the largest sense, to mitigate the harshness of all fatalities. And in the thorough recognition of that worse share, I think there is a basis for a sublimer resignation in woman and a more regenerating tenderness in man.

Here she comes out tentatively in favour of 'sublimer resignation' for women and 'more regenerating tenderness' for men. 'I do not trust very confidently to my own impressions on this subject.'

The argument continues:

> The one conviction on the matter which I hold with some tenacity is, that through all transitions the goal towards which we are proceeding is a more clearly discerned distinctness of function (allowing always for exceptional cases of individual organisation) with as near an approach to equivalence of good for woman and for man as can be secured by the effort of growing moral force to lighten the pressure of hard non-moral outward conditions.

Women and men have distinct functions. But what those functions may be are here obscure, as is the tone. Is this separatism or apartheid? That women are to be left at the mercy of their procreativity, caught between that and 'hard non-moral outward conditions' seems a melancholy upshot to her brooding. Yet how else can we read this letter?

# VI

One way is to look ahead to the activity of *Middlemarch* which brings into question again the idea of what is 'natural' in function and in attitude for women. The Victorian fascination with the concept of natural law—a reconstitution within the physical order of the older concept of design—had many consequences in the culture. It could be used to ratify socially-determined practices as if they were part of nature. Even Marx fell into this trap with his treatment of the family as a 'prior' and natural organisation. Once things are 'natural', they are seen as inevitable. And we feel, even in the letter just discussed, a tension between the repudiation of 'nature' and the embrace of 'function'.

The concept of natural law bore hard on women since it based their role on the precondition of procreativity. Moreover, as Edith Simcox observed in her study, *Natural Law*, it restored the idea of providence as 'order'. In a passage which may have George Eliot's 'pier-glass' image behind it, Edith Simcox writes of this teleological problem:

> Every one instinctively and, in a manner necessarily, regards the incidents which concern himself as really grouped in the manner in which they present themselves to his feeling—as of course they really are—though not less really in a thousand different ways, visible with equal clearness to other centres of consciousness. (Simcox, 1877, p.156)

But though 'each several mode of stringing together the actual occurrence is true—from an arbitrarily narrowed point of view', they are 'worthless as a formula for the general relations among all the things concerned'.

Is *Middlemarch* seeking 'general relations', a reconstitution of the text as natural law? The book opens by bringing into question any easy definitions of 'the nature of women'. *Middlemarch* is a novel which calls into play the 'range of relevances called the universe', all the more so for its ironic insistence that it must forgo doing so, to concentrate on the interweaving of a few 'lots'. 'Lot', with its doubled emphasis on chance and on overdetermined outcome, its entwining of the magical and the humdrum, is a crucial word for George Eliot, particularly in her later career. Silas is cast out of his community as the result of the drawing of lots. *Middlemarch* turns on that modern equivalent, voting in committee, and *Daniel Deronda* opens with Gwendolen at play.

The chanciness of propinquity and intimacy is admirably summarised in the initiating remark on the frozen stare with which we greet our neighbours at dinner. Chance meeting may become intimate involvement over time. It is a social parallel to that earlier comment on the sadness of 'the family face' in Adam Bede. In *Middlemarch*, in particular, the action of the novel reminds us that families are made by acts of choice (or what appear to the people involved to be acts of choice). Courtship and wedding is the coming together of people linked only by social acquaintance into a knitting-up of flesh and blood in childbearing.

Is the multiformity of 'lots' within the work designed ultimately to reveal a taxonomy which conditions individual women and men according to 'laws of nature'? Or is the enterprise rather that of irradiating differences, extending distinctions, and bringing under our survey the impossibility of reaching that full interpretation which must precede any attempt to describe law? 'Differences are form,' she wrote in 'Notes on Form in Art'. Can fiction allow everything to be known? Is the narrative discourse that of a privileged, all-embracing mother? Or does it display a series of 'experiments' without reaching a 'binding theory', such as Dorothea herself always hopes to discover? Is the search for 'binding theory' itself a kind of acquiescence?

*Middlemarch* works through *explanation*—passionate explanation which produces some of the same intensity as the gossip of lovers or of intimate friends, a sustained conversation which secures and surprises. But such explanation is not end-stopped, but endless. It is no wonder that she needs the focusing metaphors of microscope and telescope. The compunction bred in the reader by the long interpenetrations of *Middlemarch* may make us forget before the end of the novel the brilliant play of spirit with which the novel opens. In the first chapters we begin to read the characters through gossip, pithy cross-comments, ironic situation, and physical details of appearance. This 'coming to know' dramatises our role as that of a privileged newcomer, reading the social scene. Not only are we getting to know people, but they are getting to know each other, a process which is intensified and restricted in courtship: Sir James Chettam courts first Dorothea, then Celia; Dorothea and Casaubon ineptly try to fit each other to prior images and, somewhat later, in the already mitigated light of accumulating interconnection, we watch the courtship of Lydgate and Rosamond. The action of the novel corresponds to the reader's entry into the fiction—particularly to that subtle wooing intrinsic to George Eliot's organisation of discourse. We participate in the initiating events because they coincide with our simultaneous experiences *as readers.*

In the early books of *Middlemarch* there is an edge of treason in that intimacy offered by the insistent *voice* of the narrative. The league of reader and writer, the 'we', sometimes inveigles us into admissions we had not foreseen. At other times it forms an allegiance which deflates the characters. The contract of reader and writer appears to be between equals, yet reserves to the writing an authority beyond whose span it is not possible for the reader to function. In Comte's *Catechism* (1858) the debate is divided between the woman who enquires and the priest who answers. Here woman and priest are combined in the narrative discourse. Precisely because so many different kinds of explanation are afforded, it is hard for the reader to counter-interpret.

George Eliot's imagination, however, works in a mode which allows her to evade factitious authority and the peremptoriness of willed sequence: metaphor creates lateral understanding, the primary participation of the reader. 'Images are the brood of desire'; that image itself multiplies images, creating a familial order (images are the children or outcome of desire) summoning equally the idea of desire brooding on possibilities, or images realising desire. The urgency of metaphor, which does not so much sort as condense, gives the reader multiple routes to knowledge. It disturbs stereotypes and the fixity of 'natural law'. Our passionate coming to consciousness in the act of realising metaphor repeats the ideal activity enjoined by the book. The unforeseen discharge of new affinity which is central to metaphor is a pleasure crucial to George Eliot's language and to her narrative ordering. Metaphor is a means of 'reaching constantly at something that is near it', at qualities which elude or strain, or poignantly are debarred to us.

Her significant placing as epigraph to Chapter 1 of the passage from *The Maid's Tragedy* with which I began this chapter, has its bearing on her uses of metaphor.

Clichés and tropes which bind up experience stir again into meaning. Words yield at their boundaries. Fugitive kinship is discovered in metaphor: affinity proves to be real without needing to be permanent. George Eliot's moral sense of connectedness is eased by metaphor's double motion, towards and away from present objects and feelings. Her intensely metaphorical style offers multiple routes beyond the world of *Middlemarch* itself, discovering at once connection and difference. In that sense, metaphor can act as an alternative mode of classification, one that makes more space for divergence and possibility. Her method is different from the encyclopaedism of Rabelais or Joyce, though it calls on as full a range of learning. The gigantism of lists has little appeal for her, nor does the collapse of puns. Instead she emphasises relations.

George Eliot's impress of knowledge gives us range and freedom. Elsewhere I have discussed ways in which in *Middlemarch* the writings of Darwin and of Jameson are related in a releasing perception of lateral connections (Beer, 1983). We are not, as readers, obliged to carry the burden of her characters' disappointment without relief. We have access to a world compacted of meaning, yet so profuse that we need not even expect to raise all connections into consciousness. This quality of latency means that the exhaustiveness of explanation does not enclose or imprison text and reader. Explanation is preceded and surpassed by the condensed form of image. The drama of analysis is supplemented by the suffusive action of imagery, and the sources of that imagery range wide across human knowledge. By this means she is able to discover the intense particularity of experience in

what is common. Simultaneously she uses that particularity as the ground of generalisation, dwelling on the
common physical conditions of our life (the body, the
material world) as the matter of metaphor.

Some of the novelty of her method has vanished for
us now, as the up-to-date range of scientific allusions
sinks into familiarity or vanishes out of sight. It is with
some surprise that a present-day reader comes upon
Hutton's objection to her early description of Dorothea:

> Signs are small measurable things, but interpretations are
> illimitable, and in girls of sweet, ardent nature every sign is
> apt to conjure up wonder, hope, belief, vast as a sky, and
> coloured by a diffused thimbleful of matter in the shape of
> knowledge, (by the way, should George Eliot assume in the
> mind of her readers a knowledge of the results of Professor
> Tyndall's speculations as to the cause of the blueness of the
> sky?) (Carroll, 1971, p.287)

The 'imaginative' for her means the mind's primary
power of 'swift images' which register desire's entry into
consciousness: 'We are all of us imaginative in some
form or other, for images are the brood of desire' (Book
II, p.77). Images cross bounds, and first of all the bound
between the unconscious and language: 'these fine
words . . . are not the language in which we think.
Deronda's thinking went on in rapid images of what
might be'. (*Daniel Deronda*, I, p.308, ch.19). Barriers are
needed for naming, but must be broken for experience.
Her realism uses not only the sub-sets of classification in
which categories more and more closely divide and
articulate, but also the traversing of categories in ways
which 'measures the subtlety of those touches which
convey the quality of soul as well as body' (ch.39).

At the beginning of Chapter 37 she gives a practical
demonstration of how words subtly shift their significa-

tion according to the case they refer to. She cites as epigraph Spenser's noble sonnet which she had earlier written out in her commonplace book.

Thrice happy she that is so well assured
Unto herself, and settled so in heart,
That neither will for better be allured
Ne fears to worse with any chance to start,
But like a steddy ship doth strongly part
The raging waves, and keeps her course aright:
Ne aught for tempest doth from it depart,
Ne aught for fairer weather's false delight.
Such self-assurance need not fear the spight
Of grudging foes; ne favour seek of friends;
But in the stay of her own stedfast might
Neither to one herself nor other bends.
  Most happy she that most assured doth rest.
  But he most happy who such one loves best.

The sonnet is placed immediately after the chapter in which Rosamond has declared to Lydgate "I never give up anything that I choose to do" and he has thought how adorable is such constancy of purpose. The wedding is brought forward. The chapter ends:

> Lydgate relied much on the psychological difference between what for the sake of variety I will call goose and gander: especially on the innate submissiveness of the goose as beautifully corresponding to the strength of the gander. (II, p.216, ch.36)

Heading the page immediately after that conclusion, the poem is ironised: the 'stay of her own stedfast might' is now suspect. Lydgate misreads along the lines of traditional values. Yet the tranquillity of the sonnet also endures and offers a possibility of recuperating a fuller meaning for words which their setting demeans. Dorothea is less 'well assured' and 'settled', but the ensuing chapter suggests a new reading of the sonnet inspired by her troubled sense of justice.

The disadvantage of words, as George Eliot noted in her journal in a passage from Victor Hugo, is that they have a stricter outline than do ideas. Truth, she quoted elsewhere in her Commonplace Book, lies in nuances. In *Middlemarch* she seeks ways beyond this difficulty by means of permeating metaphors, which enact knowledge shared by author and reader. The multiplying of narratives and the manifold comparisons and divergences of human lots take us beyond dualism or the 'hierarchised opposition', as Cixous calls it, of the 'two-term system, related to the couple man/woman' (Marks and Coutivron, 1981, p.91). The constant metaphoric activity 'incorporates' the reader. One of Donne's letters, which she read as she worked on *Middlemarch*, chimed in with her own creative activity as well as with the problems that she was creating for her characters:

> Therefore I would fain do something: but that I cannot tell what, is no wonder. For to choose, is to do: but to be no part of any body, is to be nothing. At most, the greatest persons, are but great wens, and excrescences; men of wit and delightful conversation, but as moles for ornament, except they be so incorporated into the body of the world, that they contribute something to the sustenation of the whole ... [I] was diverted by the worst voluptuousness, which is an hydroptic immoderate desire of human learning and languages. (Alford, 1839, VI, p.321)

The 'hydroptic immoderate desire of human learning' is the mole-ridden Casaubon's failing perhaps, except that he does not with *sufficient* voluptuousness desire full 'human learning'. It is even more a danger for George Eliot whose polymathic discourse in *Romola* had ornamented rather than sustained the whole. In *Middlemarch*, where the crucial topic of the whole is finding satisfying work to do, George Eliot finds a way of escaping 'excrescence'. Her work is the text. She is a professional writer; but rather than setting that self apart, the novel as readding–process incorporates the activity of writing into the society of Middlemarch, from which it would otherwise be excluded. The narrative discourse does not dramatise its own 'exceptionalness': it ranges tranquilly across shared worlds. It presents its telling as reminding; it discovers insight in the reader. There is no opposition between the 'ordinary' and the 'exceptional' in this work, between Cixous's poles: 'Nature/History, Nature/Art, Nature/Mind, Passion/Action'. Both metaphor and generalisation here emphasise what is held in common: the human body, human emotions and the physical conditions of the material world which sustain and hold them in check. Her hard recognition of the shared material world is also at times playfully reversed to yield improbable connections: Mrs Cadwallader's mind is 'as active as phosphorus, biting everything that came near into the form that suited it'. The forced connection of chemical and psychological action is witty and temporary. The full physical intensity of interconnected mental and bodily life counterweights the next passage:

> And now she pictured to herself the days, and months, and years which she must spend in sorting what might be called shattered mummies, and fragments of a tradition which was itself a mosaic wrought from crushed ruins—sorting them as food for a theory which was already withered in the birth like an elfin child. Doubtless a vigorous error vigorously pursued has kept the embryos of truth a-breathing: the quest of gold being at the same time a questioning of substances, the body of chemistry is prepared for its soul, and Lavoisier is born. But Mr

Casaubon's theory of the elements which made the seed of
all tradition was not likely to bruise itself unawares against
discoveries: it floated among flexible conjectures no more
solid than those etymologies which seemed strong because
of likeness in sound until it was shown that likeness in
sound made them impossible: it was a method of interpretation which was not tested by the necessity of forming
anything which had sharper collisions than an elaborate
notion of Gog and Magog: it was as free from interruption
as a plan for threading the stars together. (II, pp.312–13,
ch.48)

The imagery of childbirth, of alchemical transformation
and of necessary questioning, of comparative grammar
and etymology, of Grimm's law, of embryos, bodies and
soul, here suggests the possibility that Casaubon's
enterprise of seeking a key to lock stories together, may
have some worth. But the loss of contact with human
sense and human sexuality (that vigorous connection
between knowledge and desire which Donne and
George Eliot both know) reveals Casaubon's enfeebled
imagination: 'but the seed of all tradition was not likely
to bruise itself unawares.' No hard surfaces, no
collisions, no necessary connections: he floats like
embryo or traveller in a space of purely fanciful
connection: 'a plan for threading the stars together'.

The idea that meant so much to George Eliot,
'incarnation'—the word made flesh—takes some of its
particular intensity and difficulty for her from childbirth. 'Incorporation' in *Middlemarch* is also a crucial
image: as Donne says, 'to be no part of any body is to be
nothing.' Sexual love and commitment to community
share in this work the same energy. 'Contributing
something to the sustenation of the whole' must be a
limiting as well as a satisfying endeavour. Lydgate ends
by feeling that 'he had not done what he once meant to

do', (III, p.495, Finale) and Dorothea by feeling 'that there was always something better which she might have done, if she had only been better and known better' (p.461). The conditions of their education, of the false relations created socially between men and women, bear a large responsibility for their sense of inadequacy or failure. But it is also a measure of the enlargement of our expectations created by the book's activity that we perceive the true power of their aspirations.

We experience the successful doctor, Lydgate, and the Member of Parliament's wife, Dorothea Ladislaw, not according to such social labels, but as mitigated failures precisely because of the high value that they have placed upon themselves. This value is sustained by the activity of the text which, through imagery and imagination, makes us join in understanding that the 'ordinary' is freighted with fullest potential. To have rescued Dorothea—or any other of her characters—from the social conditions which unyieldingly contain, would have been to sentimentalise, and to allow her readers to feel satisfied that conditions have changed sufficiently since 1830. As it is, the book forces us still to recognise exclusion, false consciousness and atomism as part of daily experience for women, and for men and women in their relations with each other. At the same time the activity of the writing incarnates human potentiality; a potentiality which here has its diffused 'origin' in a woman, Mary Ann Evans, Mrs Lewes, who has found her work: George Eliot.

## Chapter Seven

# Voice and Vengeance:
# The Poems and *Daniel Deronda*

## *I*

In her poems, particularly *The Spanish Gypsy* and
'Armgart', and in *Daniel Deronda*, George Eliot turned to
the difficulty of the exceptional woman and of women
seeking to be exceptional. 'Exceptionalness' was a moral
and a technical problem for her. The congress of genes,
environment and opportunity which makes for rare
success might seem to face her in her glass. Yet, rightly,
she never rested happy with being an exception. She
remembered the girlhood wounds of being thought
'uncanny' by other women right into her old age. She
chose to break social laws, yet wished to live an ordinary
existence. Marcia Midler comments on her 'awareness
of her own privilege' (Midler, 1980, pp. 97–108),
whereas Ellen Moers (1978) claims that she was
interested only in exceptional, 'large-souled' women.
Virginia Woolf praised her representation of demand
and utterance in all those who had been dumb:

> The ancient consciousness of woman, charged with
> suffering and sensibility, and for so many ages dumb, seems
> in them to have brimmed and overflowed and uttered a
> demand for something—they scarcely know what. (Woolf,
> 1925, p. 217)

In her review of Riehl's 'The Natural History of German
Life', George Eliot objected to idealised representations
of ordinary working people because they misled the
reader's sympathies:

> It is not so very serious that we should have false ideas about
> evanescent fashions—about the manners and conversation
> of beaux and duchesses; but it *is* serious that our sympathy
> with the perennial joys and struggles, the toil, the tragedy,
> and the humour in the life of our more heavily-laden fellow-
> men, should be perverted, and turned towards a false object
> instead of the true one. (Pinney 1963, p. 271)

Idealised representations pervert sympathy while
'appeals founded on generalizations and statistics
require a sympathy ready-made' (ibid., p. 270). George
Eliot early recognised that the exceptional changes
nothing. It carries with it no transformation of the
ordinary. By outgoing the general rule it may actually
have the effect of confirming the status quo. It is a
problem that women still live with. The exceptionally
sucessful woman is pointed to as though that demonstrated that all women are now free, and free to be
successful. George Eliot saw that it is the ordinary case
that tests the true state of affairs.

No woman in George Eliot's novels is a writer, save
Mary Garth, and her small achievement is attributed by
the Middlemarch gossips to Fred (as his is to her). In
contrast, Elizabeth Barrett Browning showed us a
woman poet in Aurora Leigh; Charlotte Brontë quite

directly and without comment made her heroines into writers by means of the form of the book: Jane and Lucy write their lives. In George Eliot's novels the nearest her women get to the writer's life is to be a reader and transcriber (Romola), or an amanuensis and research assistant (Dorothea). In her 1857 review of Holme Lee's *Kathie Brand*, George Eliot notes among the 'elements worked up into a hundred stories' the figure of 'a literary woman, who scandalises the provincial town'. No such figure ever appears even on the periphery of her books, although she was fond of using conventional characters and re-reading them. The relativism of multiple scribes, of writers within the writing, creates a self-consciousness of a kind other than she required. The multiple authors in her texts are there by means of allusion, or framed and chosen as epigraph. That is, they are all held within the range of the created writing persona, George Eliot.

Her chosen figure for the creative woman is not the writer, who might too much draw attention to George Eliot's own activity in her work. Instead it is the musician, and in particular the singer. From *Scenes of Clerical Life* through to *Daniel Deronda*, the woman singer, or the woman singing, is a recurrent and powerful figure. Ellen Moers, in *Literary Women*, comments on the feminist ideal of the opera singer: 'the miracle of operatic performance served as could no other to show off a woman's genius' (Moers, 1978, p. 189). The opera singer is musician and actress, instrument and individual.

In 'Professions for Women', years later, Virginia Woolf remarked that

> The cheapness of writing paper is, of course, the reason why women have succeeded as writers before they have succeeded in other professions . . . No demand was made on the family purse. (Woolf, 1942, p. 149)

The singer, likewise, needs to buy no instrument. She *is*
her instrument. Her gift as artist is thereby naturalised.
Armgart, in attacking 'the oft-taught Gospel' of men's
supremacy and women's subservience, is able to claim
'Nature' as peculiarly on her side.

> Yes, I know
> The oft-taught Gospel: 'Woman, thy desire
> Shall be that all superlatives on earth
> Belong to men, save the one highest kind—
> To be a mother. Thou shalt not desire
> To do aught best save pure subservience:
> Nature has willed it so!' O blessed Nature!
> Let her be arbitress; she gave me voice
> Such as she only gives a woman child,
> Best of its kind, gave me ambition too.
>
> (*Poems*, pp. 95–6)

Her voice is part of nature, and part of her *woman's*
nature, and so, consequently and equally, is her ambition
as artist.

'Voice' had always great significance for George Eliot.
The half-speaking tones in the silence of the text were a
means to authenticity, a means of sustaining ontological
presence for the writer and entry for the reader. We
remember that Dorothea was privileged with a fine,
natural speaking voice, full of assent. For the singer and
the actress voice is channelled energy, able to give fuller
expression to passionate experience and to aggression
than can be encompassed by the speaking voice of
conversation. One of the writers on music whom
George Eliot admired, John Hullah, was not only a major
historian of music from whose work she made copious
notes whose uses we can see in *Daniel Deronda*. He was
also a practical campaigner for the release of 'voice'. One
of his early works was entitled *The Duty and Advantage of*

*Learning to Sing* (1846) and he there associates the constriction of the speaking voice with the inhibitions of class-ridden English society:

> What can be easier than to speak in our *natural* voices? Nothing, certainly, were we left to the free influences of nature on the vocal organs; which influences it is the tendency of ordinary English education and habits to obstruct in every sort of way. (Hullah, 1846, p. 8)

It is as though, he suggests, 'voice' were identified with 'the most evil dispositions of our common nature'. So it was, since it is associated with power and freedom and, for women, in the medicalised vocabulary of the time, with hysteria and outrage. The outcry of Medea as she utters the name 'Jasone' is linked to the abandoned mistress Mrs Glasher, in *Daniel Deronda;* the full clarity of Dorothea demanding better conditions for workers needs the complete, not the suppressed voice. As Hullah goes on to remark:

> as to women of the higher or middle classes, what with living in hot rooms, want of exercise, and other sophistications, the majority pass through life without ever using their 'natural voices' at all. (Ibid.)

The solution he proposes is choral singing. In George Eliot's work, singing and making music together is, for amateurs, the pathway to friendship and pleasure and to fuller self-accord. Maggie Tulliver, in *The Mill on the Floss*, finds in playing the piano 'a more pregnant, passionate language'.

> The mere concord of octaves was a delight to Maggie, and she would often take up a book of studies rather than any melody, that she might taste more keenly by abstraction the more primitive sensation of intervals. (II, p. 210, Ch. 6).

The primary pleasures of music (senses and art at one) are an important register for understanding the nature of her people: Maggie did not have 'great specific talent', but rather 'sensibility to the supreme excitement of music'. The 'wildness' of Purcell attracts her, as opposed to Haydn. And those readers who complain of the slight grounds for the 'infatuation' that Maggie and Stephen experience overlook a convincing source of the feeling between them: it is voice. The mingling of voices, of duet and instrument, makes for an intensely shared physical happiness. The narrative jokingly comments on the tendency of music to draw young people together across political and social boundaries, and in *The Mill on the Floss* physical pleasure and a sharable world of art beyond the boundaries of St Ogg's is expressed in music-making.

The 'supreme excitement' of music can betray. Lydgate is misled by Rosamond's technical prowess into believing that she is the soul of the music she performs, instead of simply its drilled executant. And Gwendolen loses all pleasure in singing and playing after her rebuff by Klesmer, who opens up to her vision the gulf between 'the drawing-room *Standpunkt* and the devoted life of a professional artist'. The combination of discipline and of natural talent in the life of the musician comprises one important meaning of the figure for George Eliot. In her early essay 'Silly Novels by Lady Novelists' she had emphasised the absolute safeguards that technique afforded against self-delusion:

> Ladies are not wont to be very grossly deceived as to their power of playing on the piano; here certain positive difficulties of execution have to be conquered, and incompetence inevitably breaks down. Every art which has its absolute *technique* is, to a certain extent, guarded from the intrusions of mere left-handed imbecility. But in novel-

writing there are no barriers for incapacity to stumble against. (Pinney, 1963, p. 324)

The dedication and self-appraisal that performance requires allowed George Eliot to represent the artist's burden (and privilege) in the figure of the musician. But, the woman singer (and, more equivocally, the actress) had other and more urgent meaning in her art. The contrast between social confinement and assertive powers fuels the melodrama of 'Mr Gilfil's Love Story' in *Scenes of Clerical Life*. There, Caterina, wasting under disappointed love, still retains her talent for singing:

And her singing—the one thing in which she ceased to be passive, and became prominent—lost none of its energy. She herself sometimes wondered how it was that, whether she felt sad or angry . . . it was always a relief to her to sing. Those full deep notes she sent forth seemed to be lifting the pain from her heart—seemed to be carrying away the madness from her brain. (I, p. 250, ch. 10)

Playing 'All we like sheep' on the harpsichord, Caterina 'threw herself at once into the impetuous intricacies of that magnificent fugue . . . all the passion that made her misery was hurled by a convulsive effort into her music' (I, p. 276, ch. 13). The channelling of utterance, and of outrage, is part of music's meaning for her heroines who would otherwise be doomed to silence. Laure, Lydgate's first love in *Middlemarch*, acts out what Gwendolen in *Deronda* imagines: she stabs her husband on stage, under the protection of drama.

Ambition and vengeance can become creativity. So Walpurga says of Armgart at the beginning of the poem:

For herself,
She often wonders what her life had been

Without that voice for channel to her soul.
She says, it must have leaped through all her limbs—
Made her a Maenad—made her snatch a brand
And fire some forest, that her rage might mount
In crashing roaring flames through half a land,
Leaving her still and patient for a while
'Poor wretch!' she says, of any murderess—
'The world was cruel, and she could not sing:
I carry my revenges in my throat;
I love in singing, and am loved again.'

(*Poems*, p. 75)

The vehement connection between passion and utterance—and in particular between vengeance and singing
—recurs a number of times in George Eliot's work, and is
associated with women's desire for freedom. Laure
killed her husband because his love wearied her. Daniel
Deronda's mother asserts her right to absolute independence:

'I did not want affection. I had been stifled with it. I
wanted to live out the life that was in me, and not to be
hampered with other lives . . . I was a great singer, and I
acted as well as I sang . . . I was living a myriad of lives in
one. I did not want a child.' (III, p. 123, ch. 51)

Erinna, in George Eliot's unpublished poem of that
name, is connected with the figure of Alchirisi (or the
Princess Halm-Eberstein), Daniel's mother. Erinna was
a young woman poet in Ancient Greece, who was
chained by her mother to the spinning-wheel and died
thus, imprisoned. Her entrapment represents the fate
from which the Princess has struggled to escape. In
'Erinna' George Eliot wrote:

Hark, the passion in her eyes
Changes to melodic cries.

In the passage which she cites as epigraph to Chapter 51 of *Daniel Deronda*, Erinna sits bound

> Gazing with a sad surprise
> At surging visions of her destiny—
> To spin the byssus drearily
> In insect-labour, while the throng
> Of gods and men wrought deeds that poets wrought in
> song.
>
> (III, p. 180, ch. 51)

The voice of the woman poet or singer cries out for freedom. Here George Eliot draws on a long tradition in music and in poetry—the tradition of monody, of the Pythian voice. 'Carmina' in Ovid's *Heroides* (the poems of women seeking to recall their lovers) are the spells of the jealous Medea, a figure who haunts George Eliot's work both in *Felix Holt* and *Daniel Deronda* (Beer, 1982, pp. 125-51, 1982). The woman worsted, cast off, who can discover power only through spells and through the rhetoric of outrage, is shown in a worse dilemma in Mrs Transome, and in Mrs Glasher ('a kind of Medea and Creusa' Lush calls her and Gwendolen). Their state is worse because they have no voice. They must stay mum. Lydia Glasher makes

> a Medusa-apparition . . . vindictiveness and jealousy finding relief in an outlet of venom, though it were as futile as that of a viper already flung to the other side of the hedge. (III, p. 93)

The hideous image sympathetically gives vent to anger depraved by impotence.

The woman singer, in contrast, is powerful and creative, independent of men. In George Eliot's art there is a strong knitting up of symbolic meaning with social observation. It was indeed the case that acting and singing were the only way for women to reach individual distinction in the public arena. We think of Rachel, about whom G.H. Lewes wrote so well and who appears also in *Villette*, or Jenny Lind, towards whom George Eliot's feeling were equivocal. In an early review she cites the opinion of Henry Chorley:

> It is in the more essential attributes of the true Artist that he finds her wanting; in that self-abnegation, and devotion, and readiness to immolate personal ambition at the shrine of Art, without which all is indeed vanity and vexation of spirit. (*Leader*, 1854, vol. V, p. 403)

It is with her that Gwendolen is compared, as William J. Sullivan (1974–75), pointed out

> Her voice was a moderately powerful soprano (someone had told her it was like Jenny Lind's), her ear good, and she was able to keep in time, so that her singing gave pleasure to ordinary hearers, and she had been used to unmingled applause. (*Daniel Deronda*, I p. 66, ch. 5)

It is not surprising, therefore, that when Gwendolen realises that she must earn her living, she turns away from the dull notion of governessing, to the glamorous one of stage performance. It was, as Walter Donaldson observed:

> the only position where woman is perfectly independent of man, and where, by her talent and conduct, she obtains the favour of the public. She then enters the theatre emancipated and disenthralled from the fears and heartburning too often felt by those forced into a life of tuition and servitude. (*Fifty Years of Green-room Gossip* 1881, pp. 246–7)

But to be 'disenthralled' from the ordinary lot of women required very special talents and commitment. Of its nature, such a life emphasises the isolation of the individual performer. The artist has rights, but must exercise them in singleness. Alchirisi says, ' "Had I not a rightful claim to be something more than a mere daughter and mother? The voice and the genius matched the face" ' (III, p. 183, ch. 53). Like Armgart, her extraordinary voice determines her to overstep social convention. The problem is that thereby women artists become separated from the lot of other women and careless or ignorant of it, as Richard Simpson had accused George Eliot of doing (see p. 102). 'Armgart' powerfully explores these difficulties. There is never any suggestion that Armgart or Alchirisi should have neglected or renounced their talents: Deronda says: ' "I can imagine the hardship of an enforced renunciation" ' (III, p. 131, ch. 51), but his mother refuses that dangerous claim of empathy: ' "No", said the Princess, shaking her head, and folding her arms with an air of decision. "You are not a woman" ' (ibid.).

In her earlier books George Eliot leaves out, or peripheralises, 'communities of women' (Auerbach, 1978). Gossip provides one such community, but a community about which the narrator has mixed feelings, sharing and spurning the art. In *Daniel Deronda* most of the families studied consist of mother and daughters: Gwendolen and her sisters; the Mallingers (Lady Mallinger thinks of herself as 'the infelicitous wife who had produced nothing but daughters, little better than no children' and whose lack of a son results in Grandcourt inheriting the estates); Mrs Meyrick, who has a son but whom we see constantly at home with her daughters, to whom Mirah is added. Mrs Glasher has three daughters and a son whose faces are 'a reduction of her own'. Mothers and daughters make up the typical family unit in *Deronda*, and it is the search for the mother that fuels both dread and hope in Deronda and in Mirah. The search for satisfaction within such essentially matriarchal family communities is the dynamic of the characters' concern. The search for wider kinship across race as much as gender is the dynamic of the novel. Deronda's doubling as Englishman and Jew expresses that kinship. The concern for community is given mythic expression in the tale of the Delphic women from Plutarch that comes to Deronda's mind after he has rescued Mirah and is wondering where to take her:

> How when the Maenads, outworn with their torch-lit wanderings, lay down to sleep in the market-place, the matrons came and stood silently round them to keep guard over their slumbers; then when they waked, ministered to them tenderly, and saw them safely to their own borders. (I,p. 291, ch. 17)

Maenad and matron unite in psychic wholeness and women's solidarity—a solidarity in which Deronda longs to have a part.

The image of the woman artist as 'maenad', firing a forest 'that her rage might mount/In crashing roaring flames through half a land' introduces Armgart. The poem of that name works with impressive complexity at the problem of the 'maenad', the passional, declarative woman, essentially creative, and freed from the ordinary conditions of living as a woman. Armgart is cared for by her cousin Walpurga, the songless confidante. When Armgart first appears she has just sung Gluck's 'Orpheus'. This opera had particular meaning for George Eliot, a meaning that was involved with the practice of having a woman sing Orpheus. Orpheus goes to rescue Eurydice, and in Gluck's version, succeeds

211

(Haight, 1954, II, p. 191). In her Journal in November 1858 she records seeing the opera and writes: 'We talked about symbolism—how far it prevailed among the Greeks'. She was distrustful of music that became conscious symbol: 'music will be great and ultimately triumphant over men's ears and souls in proportion as it is less a studied than an involuntary symbol' (Pinney, 1963. p. 104). The figure of the woman singer dressed as a man, releasing the loved woman Eurydice from death by the power of her music, had a particular symbolic value for George Eliot: she too was known as a woman artist, though clad in man's name. The figure brought to the surface, also, a particular difficulty. Armgart is wooed by an aristocrat who believes, 'A woman's rank/Lies in the fulness of her womanhood'. Armgart sees the trap. He tolerates her singing, and values her because she has a gift to renounce which will add value to her private presence. She scornfully rejects that 'dispersed' life that Dorothea ends content with:

> Sing in the chimney-corner to inspire
> My husband reading news? Let the world hear
> My music only in his morning speech
> Less stammering than most honourable men's?
>
> (*Poems*, p. 97)

But disaster comes to Armgart. She loses her voice through a protracted illness. And it is at this point that a new and unexpected voice is heard. Armgart, mourning her loss and her now ordinary state, is turned on by Walpurga, the nurturing confidante. Walpurga, the songless, ordinary woman, blames Armgart for her elitism, her emphasis on her own exceptionalness, her refusal to accept 'the mighty sum/Of claims unpaid to needy myriads':

> Where is the rebel's right for you alone.
> Noble rebellion lifts a common load;
> But what is he who flings his own load off
> And leaves his fellows toiling? Rebel's right?
> Say rather, the deserter's. O, you smiled
> From your clear height on all the million lots
> Which yet you brand as abject.
>
> (*Poems*, pp. 130–1)

The privileged woman has changed nothing, it seems. Other women continue to bear their load, because they do not share the privilege of special talent. At the end, Armgart rejects the opportunity of continuing as an actress, trading on her name, and prefers to become a teacher who will train other women singers. Her voice becomes her dead child:

> O, it is hard
> To take the little corpse, and lay it low,
> And say, 'None misses it but me'.
> She sings . . .
> I mean Paulina sings Fidelio,
> And they will welcome her to-night.
>
> (*Poems*, p. 140)

Armgart's rival continues her career; there are other women singers, and Paulina, too, expresses the power of the woman singing: Fidelio, in Beethoven's opera, is a strong woman disguised as a boy, come to rescue her husband from imprisonment. In both Orpheus and Fidelio the woman takes on the role of a man, but for the audience remains known as the woman artist, and succeeds in rescuing her spouse.

## II

Armgart, rejecting 'the theory called Nature', is pro-

213

tected by her special talent. In *Daniel Deronda* George Eliot turns to exceptional fates, such as the unsought dispensation which comes to Daniel, and to the fates of those who would be exceptional, like Gwendolen.

*Daniel Deronda* is the most experimental of all George Eliot's novels—experimental in the technical sense that she tried out new narrative organisation, doing away with any pretence of accord between *sujet* and *fabula*. It is also the most experimental in its representation of new shapes for relationship.

In *Daniel Deronda* emotions find their extremest forms, sometimes appearing solidified like the Furies in Greek drama. In this book the surge of anger, vengeance and compassion keeps freezing into tableaux. She compares them to strange languages whose hieroglyphs seem to precede meaning so that we look at shapes before we give them names. The book is studded with parables: parables of fracture, sacrifice, reasserted selfhood. Violent interpretation comes from the most unexpected sources, like Mirah's perception that the woman who sacrifices her life seeks to impose herself forever on her lover. Even more than in George Eliot's previous books, parallel narratives are fleetingly condensed through allusion to opera, myth, legend, politics.

The silence in which so much of *Daniel Deronda* takes place is a terrifying seal over the crowded and various discourses of the text. Here, the process of reading is assimilated very tightly to the silent movement of thought within us. The tone of speech is lost and with it the distance between language and represented characters. The characters act out much of their experience without speech. This has the effect of intensely dramatising *encounter* when it does occur. So snatched scenes of conversation between Deronda and Gwendolen are imbued with a hieratic value. Comte's religion of humanity, in whose catechism the twinned figures are woman and priest, is akin to the vehement questioning, the pained and needed answers, which wound and yoke Deronda and Gwendolen. Deronda resents his own priest-like function. He wishes to be ordinary, but his circumstances, as much as his power of empathy, force him into exceptional positions.

By means of these activities George Eliot brings into question our assumptions about the prescribed shapes for experience. She triples the figure of the woman singer: Alchirisi, Mirah and the failed Gwendolen. The most impressive is Alchirisi, the great and isolated artist, trapped into marriage by the loss of her voice, and chafing against the constraints of ease as Princess Halm-Eberstein. She has given away her son Daniel as a small child into another culture. As in *The Spanish Gypsy*, the child is brought up, favoured, in an imperial culture and then reclaimed by those oppressed within the culture. For Deronda, the discovery that he is a Jew is liberation; for his mother being a Jew was entrapment.

Deronda sees that she wanted, by giving him up into another name and nation, to murder the patriarchal. She sought not only her own release but to annihilate the grandson of her father, the father from whom she was in flight. There can be no reconciliation between the needs of mother and son: Deronda's will to life and kinship, her will to life and singleness. Both are given their full intelligence in these, some of the finest scenes in the book. The contradiction, so starkly set out, is one that beset George Eliot in the late books. What place is left for the father?

U.C. Knoepflmacher (1975, pp. 5381) has pointed out the 'avuncular' solution in *Middlemarch*, the substitution of the weakened form of uncle for father. In *Daniel Deronda*, though fathers exist, they are Gascoigne and

Cohen, simple repositories of the ordinary in their respective cultures. The brunt of relationship is borne by mothers. Deirdre David has pointed out the arrest of Gwendolen at the stage of loving her mother in a narcissistic mode, and her consequent inability to love others. Though as David herself points out, it is dangerous to subject figures in the text to psycho-analytic process, her commentary well emphasises the bond between personal problem and political stalemate in the novel (David, 1981, pp. 176–204).

Deronda's lack of a mother has made him polymor-phic, paradoxically himself capable of mothering, though lacking always a mother for himself. Those aspects of woman's commonly imputed experience which are absent in Alchirisi (nurturing, sympathising, living in the experience of others) are highly developed in him: 'all the woman lacking in her was present in him as he said, with some tremor in his voice—"Then are we to part, and I never be anything to you?" (III, p. 176, ch. 53). Deronda's playing of the 'woman's part' allows George Eliot to isolate and analyse difficulties in the 'sympathising role' often assigned to women.

> He shrank with dislike from the loser's bitterness and the denunciatory tone of the unaccepted innovator. A too reflective and diffusive sympathy was in danger of paralysing in him that indignation against wrong and that selectness of fellowship which are the conditions of moral force. (II, p. 132, ch. 32)

While working on *Deronda* George Eliot made notes from the Kabbalah: in its original state each soul is androgynous, and is separated into male and female when it descends to earth. But some souls suffer in this isolation:

> In that case she chooses a companion soul of better fortune or more strength. The stronger of the two then becomes as

it were the mother; she carries the sickly one in her bosom & nurses her as a woman her child. (Baker, 1976, p. 112)

In the relationship between Gwendolen and Deronda, Daniel takes on the role of the mother soul. He has filled up his mother's absence by developing his own powers of nurturing. But, like his mother, Deronda later shakes himself free, leaving Gwendolen behind in order to pursue his own projects and desires. His mother has taught him the concentration of rejection.

Deronda's role would, only a little later through the work of Freud, be institutionalised as that of the therapist. But there is no role in his society which can accept transference and not see it as seduction, and no already constituted language with which to express the difference, other than that of religion.

Adultery, as Tony Tanner (1979) has well illustrated, provides the written as well as representational tension of many acts of fiction. *Romola* and *Felix Holt* alone of George Eliot's novels depend on actual adultery. *Felix Holt*, like many other Victorian novels, studies the nemesis of parenting. In *Romola* adultery is made peripheral to the book's many issues, though it happens within the represented time of the novel. In *Felix Holt* it provides the buried root of the novel's growth and retraction. But in *Middlemarch* and *Daniel Deronda* George Eliot deeply questions adultery as a sufficient model for understanding relationships. Casaubon and Grandcourt are jealous in the conventional style, but the relationships they scrutinise will not yield to conventional readings. Grandcourt's meagre imagination allows him few images beyond that of 'appearance'.

In *Middlemarch*, Dorothea, believing herself to have surprised a scene of passionate assignation between Will and Rosamond, is able imaginatively to conceive what that could mean to a marriage, because she also fully understands the longing for intimacy that adultery can satisfy and because she must for the first time recognise the full potentiality of the feeling she has for Ladislaw.

The claustrophobic busy-ness and unproductiveness of English upper-class society oppresses Gwendolen even while she becomes part of it. For on Gwendolen is placed the great burden of the novel. She has all the aspirations to freedom and independence of the Princess without any of her talent. She must make outrageous demands in order to come near what are now ordinary freedoms. There is here no possibility of independent life for a woman *without* special talents. Gwendolen feels herself exceptional, without any decided gifts, as does Deronda who is later given the gift of his Jewishness. She has at the same time a horror of making herself 'exceptional' in the limited social meaning of odd, or out of line:

> Can we wonder at the practical submission which hid her constructive rebellion? The combination is common enough ... Poor Gwendolen had both too much and too little mental power and dignity to make herself exceptional. (III, p. 91, ch. 48)

Gwendolen, like the Princess, cannot love men according to the model offered by her society. She shares the 'trace of demon ancestry' (I, p. 96, ch. 7), the hint of Melusina, the woman who turned sometimes into a serpent from the waist down and to whom George Eliot likens the Princess in her suffering. When Gwendolen plays Hermione in her early attempt to be 'a Rachelesque heroine' (I, p. 83, ch. 6), music awakes her, not to healing but to horror. Herr Klesmer's thunderous chord makes the panel drop on 'the dead face and the fleeing figure' (I, p. 85, ch. 6). Instead of the mother justified and restored, as the scene would signify in its proper narrative place at the end of *The Winter's Tale*, this truncated tableau version, carved out to emphasise Gwendolen's statuesque good looks, shows her first transfixed with fear, then reshaped into hysteria. And Klesmer's delicate compliment to her on her fine acting ('he divined that the betrayal into a passion of fear had been mortifying to her') is misinterpreted by Gwendolen as really confirming that she has a talent for acting. Passion is awakened negatively in her, and it is through rejection and through fear that she must discover herself and the world beyond her.

In Gwendolen, George Eliot makes restitution to those earlier figures such as Hetty and Rosamond excluded from her full sympathy because they could never succeed in fully sympathising with others. Gwendolen, who looks like society's ideal of the spirited young lady, is too close to Diana for comfort. She is happiest when a virgin triumphant at the archery contest. She flourishes on competition. She has no theory of her own femininity, and no sense of community with other women:

> Gwendolen was as inwardly rebellious against the restraints of family conditions, and as ready to look through obligations into her own fundamental want of feeling for them, as if she had been sustained by the boldest speculations; but she really had no such speculations, and would at once have marked herself off from any sort of theoretical or practically reforming women by satirising them. She rejoiced to feel herself exceptional; but her horizon was that of the genteel romance where the heroine's soul poured out in her journal is full of vague power, originality, and general rebellion, while her life moves strictly in the sphere of fashion. (I, p. 74, ch. 6)

She carries, therefore, the whole weight of her predicament as a woman who dislikes love-making, and comes to dislike the thought of childbearing. She resists becoming part of 'sexual selection' (Beer, 1983, pp. 210–35). She would wish for an independent and creative life, a life in which she travels like Lady Hester Stanhope, or acts like Rachel, or sings like Jenny Lind. All these actual models for women's attainment are introduced into the novel as measures for her aspirations. She does not, like Dorothea, imagine herself as a social reformer, nor does her creator imagine her as St Theresa. She rejects all such well-meaning activities.

Both Catherine Arrowsmith with her 'exasperating thoroughness in her musical accomplishment' (I, p. 72, ch. 6) and, even more, Mirah measure for us the unreality of Gwendolen's pretensions to excellence in the world of music. Equally, she has within herself no appetite for the ordinary lot of womanhood, the round of wife and mother. She is a natural gambler, doing 'nothing in particular'. The imagery of serpents, water-nixies, demons, poison, dreams of violence, surround Gwendolen with an atmosphere of the uncanny and the primitive:

> . . . the hidden rites of vengeance with which the persecuted have made a dark vent for their rage, and soothed their suffering into dumbness. Such hidden rites went on in the secrecy of Gwendolen's mind, but not with soothing effect—rather with the effect of a struggling terror. Side by side with the dread of her husband had grown the self-dread which urged her to flee from the pursuing images wrought by her pent-up impulse. (III, p.195, ch.54)

She is 'for ever trying to flee and for ever held back'. Imagery in this book moves freely between characters. The image of throttling, of neck and strangling hands, moves to and fro obsessively between the discourse associated with Grandcourt and Gwendolen.

Gwendolen shares Armgart's murderous passion, but it is in a different sense that she 'carries her revenges in her throat'. As a child she had strangled the canary whose song annoyed her. Now 'If that idea which was maddening her had been a living thing, she would have wanted to throttle it without waiting to pose what would come of the act' (III, p. 59, ch. 48). The reader shares 'her entanglement in those fatal meshes which are woven within more closely than without' (III, p.188, ch.54). The clandestine world of seething impulse which occupies this book leaves no gaps for the reader to emerge and no vantage point from which to survey. The demonic in Gwendolen has no creative issue—except self-creation. But it fires the work. She figures woman's absolute distress. On the face of it, she is privileged, even pampered, though her need of money and independence leads her into a marriage which she knows she should not undertake. She claims life for herself without the special permission granted to talent.

It is the breaking of the bond between maenad and matron—between Gwendolen and Mrs Glasher—which disrupts the psychic world of the novel. The way out for her is not through loving another (why should we call what she feels for Deronda love?) but through needing another. She is fortunate to find, for a creative while, in Deronda, another person capable of acting and feeling outside stereotypes. This discovery leaves her at the end capable of free-standing life, no longer domineering like Alchirisi who analyses her own insistent lack of feeling:

> 'Oh yes', she answered, as to a question about a matter of course, while she folded her arms again. 'But,' . . . she added in a deeper tone, . . . 'I am not a loving woman. That is the truth. It is a talent to love—I lacked it. Others have loved me—and I have acted their love. I know very well what love

makes of men and women—it is subjection. It takes another for a larger self, enclosing this one,'—she pointed to her own bosom. 'I was never willingly subject to any man. Men have been subject to me." ' (III, p.185, ch.53)

Gwendolen is distinguished from those earlier heroines—Hetty, Bertha, Rosamond, with their physical allure—because she adds to allure imagination. She can imagine her own corruption, and in prophetic leaps experiences evil not as impulse only but as deed. That shocked, febrile awakening of the self to its own powers and the discovery that they may not be good, makes Gwendolen a powerful critique of the idealised woman.

Gwendolen demands ordinary freedoms but must make extraordinary claims to reach them. In that sense she is George Eliot's most radical representation of the oppressiveness of women's lot. The form 'we', so predominant in *Middlemarch*, with its suggestion of succour as well as constraint, is here replaced by authoritative imagery and questioning.

The imagery of singing becomes self-enclosed, allied with madness: 'to defer thought in this way was something like trying to talk down the singing in her own ears' (III, p.87, ch.48). Passion and thought become one: 'Everything is porous to it.' 'What could she say to justify her flight? . . . How was she to begin? What was she to say that would not be a condemnation of herself?' Such stark questioning has the clarity of obsession. In Gwendolen, as throughout *Deronda*, George Eliot draws on much earlier models in her own and other people's writing, and persistently flouts them.

The tradition of women's writing in England during the eighteenth and nineteenth centuries is marked by scepticism about fiction's apparently liberating dreams —both the dream-fulfilments desired by the characters within the fiction and the dream liberties offered by the text to the reader. In her early essay, 'Silly Novels by Lady Novelists', for example, George Eliot pinpoints the self-gratifying perfection attributed to the heroine in what she calls 'the mind-and-millinery species' of novel:

> Her eyes and her wit are both dazzling; her nose and her morals are alike free from any tendency to irregularity; she has a superb *contralto* and a superb intellect; she is perfectly well-dressed and perfectly religious; she dances like a sylph, and reads the Bible in the original tongues.... The men play a very subordinate part by her side. (Pinney, 1963, p. 302)

This last novel, *Daniel Deronda*, offers a daemonic deconstruction of this dream in the figures of Gwendolen Harleth trapped into a sadistic marriage by her will to dazzle and in the extraordinary powers of Alchirisi which isolate her from others.

Gwendolen, trapped by other people's expectations and by her own appetite for admiration, yet survives. Emma Bovary, always alluded to in Gwendolen, presages a harsher outcome, which George Eliot rejects. That is no mean achievement. This time the woman does not trivialise or poison herself. She does not drown, does not renounce, does not sacrifice herself. With Deronda as midwife, she achieves the birth of a liveable identity, not one that accords with her earlier expectations, or with her society's ideals, not one that will renew the world, or become part of the authority of descent. The single ego is intransigent: 'I mean to live.' We cannot know whether she is capable of sustaining that meaning. The book closes, and deliberately estranges the reader from her future. Here nothing is docketed. We are given none of the satisfaction of retrospect. Instead, we are left with the dangerous power of the uncharted future.

In Gwendolen, George Eliot creates a new kind of heroine, neither Antigone nor Madonna. She is chastened to an understanding of the common lot of women and no longer wonders at her mother's dullness. She discovers that 'not acting as other women do' may not in itself be creative. She does not marry Deronda, and must accept that she is peripheral to his plot. But she does not desire a 'proper scale' like Mirah with her perfect chamber music voice and her satisfaction with a private and supporting role. Through all this, the work sustains her. Her survival is emphasised by another strange set of allusions.

At the centre of *Clarissa* comes the rape. Lovelace next day writes laconically to Belford: 'And, now, Belford, I can go no farther. The affair is over. Clarissa lives' (VI, p. 75). Deronda is a confessor but also 'a kind of Lovelace' who makes the women run after *him*, so Sir Hugo says. He eventually abandons Gwendolen, revealing that he is a Jew, that he will leave England, and that he intends to marry. Throughout their friendship he has secretly been imaginatively bound to another: "I am cruel too, I am cruel", he repeated, with a sort of groan, looking up at her imploringly' (III, p.401, ch.69). Gwendolen repeats obsessionally variations on her last words to Deronda: ' "I will try—try to live" ' (p.403).

> 'Gwendolen, dearest, you look very ill,' she said, bending over her and touching her cold hands.
> 'Yes, mamma. But don't be afraid. I am going to live,' said Gwendolen, bursting out hysterically . . .
> Through the day and half the night she fell continually into fits of shrieking, but cried in the midst of them to her mother, 'Don't be afraid. I shall live. I mean to live.'
> After all, she slept; and when she waked in the morning light, she looked up fixedly at her mother and said tenderly, 'Ah, poor mamma! You have been sitting up with me. Don't be unhappy. I shall live. I shall be better.' (Ibid.)

Forms and statements both contribute to our reception of a work of fiction, and sometimes they are at odds with each other, as at times they are in *Deronda*. It would be unreal to suggest that forms (sequences, structures, assemblages, omissions) can present an autonomous meaning, independent of story content or totally at variance with it. Manifest content has meaning and cannot be obliterated or treated simply as adversary. The things that happen and the figures they happen to matter in our appraisal of the work's meaning. This may seem to be labouring the obvious, but in our perception that formalism unlocks hidden significance, and in our eagerness to move beneath a work's surface, there is a temptation to suggest that by *being* hidden, or by being deep, some special guarantee is given that the reader has truly unlocked the text. That is to reconstitute single reading on the obverse side of the paper. Clarissa is doomed to die: the amount of creative space accorded to the woman does not make it easily a feminist work. What *happens* to Clarissa and to Gwendolen, matters too. The creative vacillation of a work like *Daniel Deronda*, with its two-way movement (back towards origins; away from origins out into an undescribable future) achieves effects of radicalism largely by *refusing* to recount. Gwendolen is given little quarter within its pages; the events of the book make her helplessly dependent on a man who keeps his distance and yet oppresses her sadistically, and on a man who moves away from her, albeit in pity. The fate of Daniel's mother makes her a sad representative of freed women; the fate of Gwendolen leaves us without confidence in her power to sustain motives for independence. So the conclusion of content tends to one sort of meaning but the process of content sustains another. The representations of the Princess and Gwendolen write into the text the range of their desires, the intensity of their squandered lives, and this range and intensity cannot be expunged.

> 'Oh—the reasons for our actions!' said the Princess, with a ring of something like sarcastic scorn. 'When you are as old as I am, it will not seem so simple a question—"Why did you do this?" People talk of their motives in a cut and dried way. Every woman is supposed to have the same set of motives, or else to be a monster. I am not a monster, but I have not felt exactly what other women feel—or say they feel, for fear of being thought unlike others. When you reproach me in your heart for sending you away from me, you mean that I ought to say I felt about you as other women say they feel about their children. I did *not* feel that. I was glad to be freed from you. But I did well for you, and I gave you your father's fortune. (III, p.127, ch.51)

The book ends with the death of Mordecai, but that fierce will to survive, the clasp on life that Gwendolen reaches, has a connection with Richardson's conclusion. We might more readily have associated Daniel Deronda with Sir Charles Grandison, the good hero, but there is wisdom in the work's suggestion that he first succours and then violates Gwendolen by abandoning her. Unlike Richardson, though, there is at the end of *Daniel Deronda* a living heroine. Clarissa chooses death, Gwendolen life. Each is sustained by will and imagination. And Deronda is neither blamed nor, like Lovelace, made the work's principal narrative source of pleasure.

In this book, deeds lose their names, and relationships their easy contours. Vengeance fuels the action—the vengeance of Mrs Glasher against Gwendolen and Grandcourt, of the Princess against her father, of Gwendolen against Grandcourt. But vengeances are also outlived and forgone. In that other relationship of

Mordecai and Deronda, which imposes on Deronda the duty to become his friend's spiritual son and successor, there is the same radical stirring up of our assumptions about relationship, within kin and across gender, that George Eliot sought throughout this extraordinarily exploratory work.

Her conservatism and her extremism are here set in tension. The work potentiates questioning of the links between sexual relations and historical cultures, and the survival of those cultures. In *Middlemarch* she achieved a way out of the mere contradiction of male and female through multiformity. Here she does so through prophecy and through an insistence on preserving secrets. Our not knowing at the end is not ignorance, but relies on our no longer being able to rest in moral assumptions about the 'nature of woman' or the 'descent of man'. The book explores the capacities of human beings to work outside assigned sex roles and kin roles. Grandcourt and Lush work as a sick parody on Mordecai and Deronda: one acts as the agent and alter-ego of the other. Equally, Deronda is son to Mordecai, and mother to Gwendolen, while she is both husband and child to her mother. In this work George Eliot constantly sets side by side the delusive, the visionary, the corrupted, and the barely possible escape. Gwendolen escapes the marriage market. Deronda escapes British culture and British manhood, though his success in his Zionist endeavour would have seemed far less certain for the first readers (and the author) than it may do now. He, like Gwendolen, is left on an uncertain edge of possibility.

Extraordinary things happen. And it proves, in the end, that it is not only the supremely talented who can break the mould of expectation. Gwendolen and Deronda, without special talents, except those of fear and empathy which disturb sexual stereotypes and cultural fixity, are drawn into 'the pressure of a vast mysterious movement'. If that movement is simply the pull of history towards the period beyond George Eliot's own need and knowledge—no meliorist prophecy—that is part of the power of this singularly dark and glittering work.

# Bibliography

Louis Aimé-Martin, *The Education of Mothers of Families; or, The Civilisation of the Human Race by Women* (London: Whittaker/Edinburgh: A. & C. Black, 1842).

Flavia Alaya, 'Victorian Science and the "Genius" of Woman', *Journal of the History of Ideas,* 38 (1977), 261–280.

*The Alexandra Magazine,* vols 1–2 (London: Jackson, Walford & Hodder, 1864–65).

Henry Alford (ed.), *The Works of John Donne, D.D., Dean of Saint Paul's, 1621–1631, With a Memoir of His Life,* (London: John W. Parker, 1839).

Anon., 'Social Science', *Blackwood's Edinburgh Magazine,* 90 (1861), 463–78.

*The Arabian Nights Entertainments,* 4 vols (London: C.D. Piguenit, 1792).

Isobel Armstrong, *Middlemarch*: A note on George Eliot's Wisdom', in *Critical Essays on George Eliot,* ed. Barbara Hardy (London: Athlone Press/New York: Barnes & Noble, 1970)

Nina Auerbach, *Woman and the Demon: The Life of a Victorian Myth,* (Cambridge, Mass.; London: Harvard University Press, 1982).

Zelda Austen, 'Why Feminist Critics are Angry with George Eliot', *College English*, 37 (1976), 549–61.

William Baker (ed.), *Some George Eliot Notebooks*, (an edition of the Carl H. Pforzheimer Library's George Eliot Holograph Notebooks, MSS 707–7), vol. 1—MS 707, (Salzburg: Institut für Englische Spräche und Literatur, Universität Salzburg, 1976.)

Linda Bamber, 'Self-Defeating Politics in George Eliot's *Felix Holt*', *Victorian Studies*, 18 (1975), 419–35.

Michele Barrett, *Women's Oppression Today: Problems in Marxist Feminist Analysis* (London: Verso Editions/NLB, 1980).

Elizabeth Barrett Browning, *Aurora Leigh* (London: Chapman & Hall, 1857).

Françoise Basch, *Relative Creatures: Victorian Women in Society and the Novel, 1837–67*, tr. A. Rudolf (London: Allen Lane, 1974).

Simone de Beauvoir, *The Second Sex*, tr. & ed. H.M. Parshley (Harmondsworth: Penguin Books, 1972).

Gillian Beer, 'Beyond Determinism: George Eliot and Virginia Woolf', in *Women Writing and Writing about Women*, ed. Mary Jacobus (London: Croom Helm, 1979) pp.80–99.

———, ' "Our Unnatural No-Voice": The Heroic Epistle, Pope, and Women's Gothic', *The Yearbook of English Studies*, 12 (1982), 125–51.

———, *Darwin's Plot: Evolutionary Narrative in Darwin, George Eliot and Nineteenth-Century Fiction* (London, Boston: Routledge & Kegan Paul, 1983)

Kathleen Blake, '*Middlemarch* and the Woman Question', *Nineteenth-Century Fiction*, 31 (1976), 285–312.

———, '*Armgart*—George Eliot on the Woman Artist', *Victorian Poetry*, 18, (1980), 75–80.

Mathilde Blind, *George Eliot* (1883) 'The Political Evolution of Women', *Westminster Review*, 134 (1890), 1–8.

———, *The Ascent of Man* (London: Chatto 1888).

Barbara (Leigh Smith) Bodichon *An American Diary 1857-8* ed J. Reed London 1972

Bibliography

Barbara (Leigh Smith) Bodichon, *A Brief Summary in Plain Language of the Most Important Laws Concerning Women*, (London, 1854).
————, *Women and Work* (London: Bosworth & Harrison, 1857).
————, 'Authorities and Precedents for Giving the Suffrage to Qualified Women', *The Englishwoman's Review* (January 1867), 63–75.
Felicia Bonaparte, *Will and Destiny: Morality and Tragedy in George Eliot's Novels* (New York: University Press, 1975).
————, *The Triptych and the Cross* (Brighton: Harvester/ New York: University Press, 1979).
Emilia Jessie Boucherett, *Hints on Self Help: A Book for Young Women* (London, 1863).
Muriel Bradbrook, 'Barbara Bodichon, George Eliot and the Limits of Feminism', James Bryce Memorial Lecture delivered in the Wolfson Hall, Somerville College, Oxford, 6 March 1975.
Patrick Brantlinger, *The Spirit of Reform: British Literature and Politics, 1832–1867* (Cambridge, Mass. and Harvard, 1977).
Fredrika Bremer, *Father and Daughter: A Portraiture from the Life*, tr. Mary Howitt (London: Arthur Hall, Virtue, 1859).
————, *Hertha* (London, 1856).
Sandra Burman (ed.), *Fit Work for Women* (London: Croom Helm, 1979).
Hester Burton, *Barbara Bodichon, 1827–1891* (London: John Murray, 1949).
David Carroll (ed.), *George Eliot: The Critical Heritage* (London: Routledge & Kegan Paul, 1971).
John Chapman, 'The Position of Woman in Barbarism and Among the Ancients', *The Westminster Review*, 64 (1855), 378–436.
Cynthia Chase, 'The Decomposition of the Elephants: Double-Reading *Daniel Deronda*', *PMLA*, 93 (1978), 215–27.

Nancy Chodorow, *The Reproduction of Mothering: Psycho-Analysis and the Sociology of Gender* (Berkeley, Los Angeles and London: University of California Press, 1978).

Carol Christ, 'Aggression and Providential Death in George Eliot's Fiction', *Novel*, 9 (1976), 130-40.

—Hélène Cixous, *La jeune née* (Paris: Union Générale d'Editions, 1975).

K.K. Collins, 'G.H. Lewes Revised: George Eliot and the Moral Sense', *Victorian Studies*, 21 (1978), 463-92.

Auguste Comte, *The Catechism of Positive Religion,* tr. Richard Congreve (London: John Chapman, 1858).

Jill Conway, 'Stereotypes of Femininity in a Theory of Sexual Evolution', *Victorian Studies* 14 (1970), 47-62.

Caroline Frances Cornwallis, 'Capabilities and Disabilities of Women', *The Westminster Review*, 67 (January 1857), 42-72.

———, 'The Property of Married Women', *The Westminster Review*, 66 (October 1856), 331-60.

Deirdre David, *Fictions of Resolution in Three Victorian Novels: 'North and South', 'Our Mutual Friend', 'Daniel Deronda'* (London and Basingstoke: Macmillan, 1981).

Emily Davies, *The Higher Education of Women* (London and New York: Alexander Strahan, 1866).

Dorothy Dinnerstein, *The Rocking of the Cradle, and the Ruling of the World* (London: Souvenir Press, 1978)

Lee R. Edwards, 'Women, Energy, and *Middlemarch'*, *Massachussets Review*, 13 (1972), 223-38.

George Eliot, *The Works of George Eliot,* Cabinet edn, 20 vols (Edinburgh and London: William Blackwood, 1878-85).

Sarah Ellis, *The Women of England, Their Social Duties and Domestic Habits* (London: Fisher, 1838).

Edward W. Ellsworth, *Liberators of the Female Mind: The Shirreff Sisters, Education Reform, and the Women's Movement* (Westport, Connecticut and London: Greenwood Press, 1979).

Jean Elshtain, *The Family in Political Thought* (Amherst: University of Massachussetts Press/Brighton: Harvester, 1982);

———, *Public Man, Private Woman, Women in Social and Political Thought* (Oxford, 1981).

Friedrich Engels, *The Origin of the Family, Private Property and the State* (London: Lawrence & Wishart, 1972; first edn, 1884).

*The Englishwoman's Journal*, vols 1–12 (London, 1857–63; incorp. with *The Alexandra Magazine*).

*The Englishwoman's Review, A Journal of Woman's work* (London, 1866–1910).

Elizabeth D. Ermarth, 'Incarnations: George Eliot's Conception of "Undeviating Law" ', *Nineteenth-Century Fiction*, 29 (1974) 273–86;

———, 'Maggie Tulliver's Long Suicide', *Studies in English Literature*, 14 (1974).

———, *Realism and Consensus in the English Novel* (Princeton, N.J.: Princeton University Press, 1983).

Louis Étienne, review of 'The Spanish Gypsy', in *Revue de Deux Mondes*, 92 (1870), 429–46.

Josette Féral, 'Antigone or *The Irony of the Tribe*', *Diacritics*, 8 (1978), 2–14.

Lloyd Fernando, 'Special Pleading and Art in *Middlemarch*: The Relations Between the Sexes', *The Modern Language Review*, 67 (1972), 44–9.

Ludwig Feuerbach, *The Essence of Christianity*, tr. Marian Evans (London: John Chapman, 1854).

Michel Foucault, *The History of Sexuality, vol. 1 An Introduction* (London: Allen Lane, 1979).

Sigmund Freud, 'Femininity', in *The Complete Introductory Lectures on Psychoanalysis*, tr. and ed. James Strachey (London: George Allen & Unwin, 1971), 576–99.

Steven W. Fullom, *The History of Woman, And her Connexion with Religion, Civilization, and Domestic Manners, from the earliest Period*, 2 vols (London: Longman, Brown, Green, and Longmans, 1855).

Jane Gallop, *Feminism and Psychoanalysis: The Daughter's Seduction* (London and Basingstoke: Macmillan 1982).

Sandra M. Gilbert and Susan Gubar, *The Madwoman in the Attic* (New Haven and London: Yale University Press, 1979).

Carol Gilligan, *In a Different Voice: psychological theory and women's development* (Cambridge, Mass. and London, Harvard University Press 1982).

Michael Ginsburg, 'Pseudonym, Epigraphs, and Narrative Voices: *Middlemarch* and the Problem of Authorship', *ELH*, 47 (1980), 542–58.

Maria Georgina Grey [Mrs William Grey], 'On the Education of Women', paper read at the Meeting of the Arts, 31 May 1871 (London: William Ridgway, 1871).

Susan Gubar, 'Mother, Maiden, and the Marriage of Death: Women Writers and an Ancient Myth', *Women's Studies*, 6 (1979), 301–15.

Gordon Haight, (ed.), *The George Eliot Letters*, 9 vols (New Haven and London: Yale University Press, 1954–78).

Gordon Haight, *George Eliot: A Biography* (Oxford, London and New York: Oxford University Press, 1978; 1st edn, 1968).

Barbara Hardy, *The Novels of George Eliot* (London: Athlone Press, 1959).

———, *Critical Essays on George Eliot* (London: Athlone Press/New York: Barnes & Noble, 1970).

Leslie Hume Hellerstein and Karen Offen (eds), *Victorian Women: a documentary account on women's lives in nineteenth-century England, France, and the United States* (Stanford: Stanford University Press/Brighton: The Harvester Press, 1981).

Gertrude Himmelfarb, *Victorian Minds* (London: Weidenfeld & Nicolson, 1968).

Patricia Hollis, (ed.), *Women in Public, 1850–1900: Documents of the Victorian Women's Movement*, (London: Allen & Unwin, 1979.

John P. Hullah, *The Duty and Advantage of Learning to Sing. A Lecture* (London, 1846).

Luce Irigaray, *Ce sexe qui n'en est pas un* (Paris: Minuit,

1977).

Mary Jacobus (ed.), *Women Writing and Writing about Women* (London: Croom Helm, 1979).

Mary Jacobus, 'The Question of Language: Men of Maxims and *The Mill on the Floss*', *Critical Inquiry*, 8 (1981), 207–22.

Henry James, *French Poets and Novelists* (London: Macmillan, 1878).

Anna Jameson, *Memoirs and Essays: Illustrative of Art, Literature, and Social Morals* (London: Richard Bentley, 1846).

——, *Sacred and Legendary Art*, 2 vols (London: Longman Brown, Green, and Longmans, 1848).

——, *Legends of the Madonna, as presented in the fine arts* (London: Longman, Brown, Green and Longmans, 1852).

Richard Jenkyn, *The Victorians and Ancient Greece* (Oxford: Oxford University Press, 1980).

Geraldine E. Jewsbury, *Constance Herbert*, 3 vols, (London: Hurst & Blackett, 1855).

Peggy Kamuf, 'Writing Like a Woman', in *Women and Language in Literature and Society*, ed. Sally McConnel-Ginet, Ruth Barker and Nelly Furman (New York: Praeger, 1980).

Cora Kaplan, 'Radical Feminism and Literature: Rethinking Millett's *Sexual Politics*', *Red Letters*, 9 (1979), 4–16.

Nannerl Keohane *et al.* (eds), *Feminist Theory: A Critique of Ideology* (Brighton: Harvester, 1982).

Arnold Kettle, 'Felix Holt the Radical', in *Critical Essays on George Eliot*, ed. Barbara Hardy (London: Routledge & Kegan Paul, 1970), 108–10.

U.C. Knoepflmacher, *George Eliot's Early Novels: The Limits of Realism*, Berkeley, Los Angeles and London: University of California Press, 1968).

——, '*Middlemarch*: an Avuncular View', *Nineteenth-Century Fiction*, 30 (1975), 53–81.

William E.H. Lecky, *History of European Morals, from*

*Augustus to Charlemagne*, 2 vols (London: Longmans, Green, 1869).

G.H. Lewes, 'The Lady Novelists', *Westminster Review*, 58 (1852), 129–41.

——, 'Auguste Comte', *Fortnightly Review*, 3 (1866), 402–4.

——, *The Physical Basis of Mind*, *(Problems of Life and Mind* 2nd series) (London: Trübner, 1877).

——, 'George Eliot's Hypothesis of Reality', *Nineteenth-Century Fiction*, 35 (1980)

——, *The Realistic Imagination* (Chicago: Chicago University Press, 1981).

Eliza Lynn Linton, *My Literary Life* (London: Hodder & Stoughton, 1899).

Karen B. Mann, 'George Eliot and Wordsworth: the power of sound and the power of mind', *SEL,*20 (1980), 675–94

——, 'George Eliot's Language of Nature: production and consumption', *ELH*, 48 (1981), 190–216.

Elaine Marks and Isabelle de Courtivron (eds), *New French Feminisms: An Anthology* (Brighton: Harvester, 1981).

Henry Maine, *Ancient Law: its connection with the early history of society and its relation to modern ideas* (London: John Murray, 1861).

Harriet Martineau, 'Female Industry', *The Edinburgh Review* (April 1859), 293–336 (London: Longman, Brown, Green, Longmans and Roberts/Edinburgh: A.C. Black, 1802–1929).

The Marxist-Feminist Literature Collective, 'Women's Writing: *Jane Eyre, Shirley, Villette, Aurora Leigh'*, *Ideology and Consciousness*, 3 (1978).

K.A. McKenzie, *Edith Simcox and George Eliot* (London: Oxford University Press, 1961).

Marcia Midler, 'George Eliot's Rebels: portraits of the artist as a woman', *Women's studies*, 7 (1980), 97–108.

Rosalind Miles, *The Fiction of Sex: themes and functions of sex difference in the modern novel* (New York, 1974).

John Stuart Mill, *The Subjection of Women* (London:

Longmans, Green, Reader, and Dyer, 1869).

J. Hillis Miller, 'Optic and Semiotic in *Middlemarch*', in *The Worlds of Victorian Fiction*, ed. Jerome Buckley (Cambridge, Mass.: Harvard University Press, 1975), 125–45.

Nancy Miller, *The Heroine's Text: Readings in the French and English Novel* (New York: Columbia University, 1980).

Kate Millett, *Sexual Politics* (London: Abacus, 1972).

John D. Milne, *Industrial and Social Position of Women, in the middle and lower ranks* (London: Chapman & Hall, 1857).

———, *Industrial Employment of Women, in the Middle and Lower Ranks*, rev. edn, (London: Longmans, Green, 1870).

Juliet Mitchell, *Psychoanalysis and Feminism* (Harmondsworth: Pelican Books, 1975).

Juliet Mitchell and Anne Oakley (eds), *The Rights and Wrongs of Women* (Harmondsworth: Penguin Books, 1976).

Sally Mitchell, *The Fallen Angel: Chastity, Class and Women's Reading 1835–1880*, (Bowling Green, Ohio: Bowling Green University Popular Press, 1981).

Ellen Moers, *Literary Women* (first published in Great Britain by W.H. Allen) London: 1977 (London: The Women's Press, 1978).

Sydney Owenson Morgan, *Woman and her Master*, 2 vols (London: Henry Colburn, 1840).

Bernard Paris, 'George Eliot's Unpublished Poetry', *Studies in Philology*, 56 (1959), 539–58.

———, 'The Inner Conflicts of Maggie Tulliver: A Horneyan Analysis', *Centennial Review* 13 (1969), 166–99.

Bessie Rayner Parkes, *Essays on Women's Work* (London: Alexander Strahan, 1965). Reviewed in *The Alexandra Magazine*, (June 1865), 371–4.

Nancy Pell, 'The Fathers' Daughters in *Daniel Deronda*', *Nineteenth-Century Fiction*, 36 (1982), 424–51.

Thomas Pinney (ed.), *Essays of George Eliot* (London: Routledge & Kegan Paul, 1963).

Thomas Pinney, 'More Leaves from George Eliot's

Notebook', *Huntington Library Quarterly*, 29 (1966), 353–76.

John C. Pratt and Victor A. Neufeldt (eds.) *George Eliot's 'Middlemarch' Notebooks: A Transcription* (Berkeley, Los Angeles and London: University of California Press, 1979).

Otto Rank, *The Myth of the Birth of the Hero* (1914; reprinted London: Vintage Books, 1964).

Ruby Redinger, *George Eliot: The Emergent Self* (London, Sydney and Toronto: The Bodley Head, 1976; first published New York: Knopf, 1975).

Mrs Hugo Reid, *A Plea for Woman: Being a Vindication of the Importance and Extent of her Natural Sphere of Action* (Edinburgh: William Tait/London: Simpkin, Marshall/ Dublin: John Cumming, 1843).

Adrienne Rich, *Of Woman Born* (New York: Bantam Books, 1977).

Samuel Richardson, *Clarissa Harlowe* (First published in 1747–48); 9 vols (London: Chapman & Hall, 1902).

Christopher Ricks, 'Female and Other Impersonators', *New York Review of Books*, 15 (July 1980).

Dianne F. Sadoff, *Monsters of Affection: Dickens, Eliot, and Brontë on Fatherhood* (Baltimore and London: Johns Hopkins University Press, 1982).

Emily Shirreff, *Intellectual Education, and its influence on the Character and Happiness of Women* (London: John W. Parker & Son, 1856).

Emily Shirreff and Maria G. Grey [nee Shirreff], *Thoughts on Self-Culture: Addressed to Women*, 2 vols, (London: Edward Moxon, 1850; page references are to the 1854 edn).

Elaine Showalter, *A Literature of Their Own: British Women Novelists from Bronte to Lessing* (Princeton, N.J.: Princeton University Press, 1977).

———, 'The Greening of Sister George', *Nineteenth-Century Fiction*, 35 (1980), 292–311.

Sally Shuttleworth, *George Eliot and Nineteenth-Century Science: The Make-believe of a Beginning* (Cambridge:

Cambridge University Press, 1984).

Edith Simcox, *Natural Law: An Essay in Ethics* (London: Trübner, 1877)

——, *Autobiography of a Shirt Maker* (MS. Bodleian Library Oxford).

Leslie Stephen, *George Eliot* (London: Macmillan, 1902).

William J. Sullivan, 'The Allusion to Jenny Lind in *Daniel Deronda*', *Nineteenth-Century Fiction*, 29 (1974–75), 211–14.

Tony Tanner, *Adultery in the Novel* (Baltimore and London: Johns Hopkins University Press, 1979).

Patricia Thomson, *George Sand and the Victorians: Her Influence and Reputation in Nineteenth-Century England* (London and Basingstoke: Macmillan, 1977).

Helen Taylor, 'Public Opinion on Questions Concerning Women', *The Englishwoman's Review* (July 1867), 223–31.

Martha Vicinus, *Suffer and Be Still: Women in the Victorian Age*, (Bloomington and London: Indiana University Press, 1972).

*Victoria Magazine* (1863–80).

Martha S. Vogeler, 'George Eliot and the Positivists', *Nineteenth-Century Fiction*, 35 (1980), 406–31.

Joseph Wiesenfarth, *George Eliot's Mythmaking* (Heidelberg: C. Winter Universitätsverlag, 1977).

Judith Wilt, *Ghosts of the Gothic: Austen, Eliot, and Lawrence* (Princeton, N.J.: Princeton University Press, 1980).

Hugh Witemeyer, *George Eliot and the Visual Arts* (New Haven and London: Yale University Press, 1979).

Virginia Woolf, *The Death of the Moth and Other Essays* (London: The Hogarth Press, 1942).

——, 'George Eliot', in *The Common Reader*, First Series (London: The Hogarth Press, 1925), 205–18.

W. Wordsworth and S.T. Coleridge, *Lyrical Ballads, 1798* edn with additional 1800 poems and Prefaces, ed. R.L. Brett and A.R. Jones (London: Methuen, 1963).

Bonnie Zimmerman, '*Felix Holt* and the True Power of Womanhood', *ELH*, 46 (1979), 432–51.

———, ' "The Mother's History" in George Eliot's Life and Political Ideology', in *The Last Tradition: Mothers and Daughters in Literature,* ed. Cathy N. Davidson and E.M. Broner (New York: Frederick Ungar, 1980), 81–94.

# Index